Constitutional responses to paradigmatic shifts in technology

Noel Cox

Ardwyn House Publishing, Aberystwyth

ISBN: 1496062388
ISBN-13: 978-1496062383

DEDICATION

To Katy, whose support, patience and understanding are always appreciated.

CONTENTS

PREFACE

The technological revolution affecting the global economy has profound implications not merely for society, but also for global and national legal systems. This work short considers the nature of the constitutional responses to paradigmatic shifts in technology. It considers the nature of constitutions and of their relationship with technology. It then proceeds to briefly examine several seminal technological changes in the past, in order to identify common elements in relation to constitutions and technology. It then looks at several contemporary technological revolutions, with a similar purpose. Finally, it seeks to draw some common themes from these examples, with the intention of identifying some lessons to guide law and policy-makers.

INTRODUCTION

The world is in the midst of a new Industrial Revolution.[1] This is a technological[2] revolution, one which is seeing seminal advances across a multitude of disciplines, and linked – if linked at all – by the distinction of belonging to what has been called the "knowledge revolution."[3] This revolution is based on the acquiring, processing, and dissemination of knowledge, just as the last great technological revolution, the Industrial Revolution, concerned the mass production, and distribution of commodities.[4] This new revolution brings with it challenges to legal

---

[1]"New" is relative. The late twentieth century has seen a range of highly significant technological advances, but some of these may be traced to the Industrial Revolution. In the nineteenth century there were also major societal, and constitutional changes, wrought by technological change; See DAVID DUNSTAN, GOVERNING THE METROPOLIS: POLITICS, TECHNOLOGY AND SOCIAL CHANGE IN A VICTORIA CITY: MELBOURNE (1984). For an African parallel see JACK GOODY, TECHNOLOGY, TRADITION AND THE STATE IN AFRICA (1980). Generally, see Steven Puro, *Technology, politics and the new Industrial Revolution*, 4 PUBL. L. FORUM 387-398 (1985); Thom W. Rudin, *State involvement in the 'new Industrial Revolution'*, 4 PUBL. L. FORUM 411-417 (1985).
[2]Here "technology" is defined broadly as processes and things people create for the purpose of using them to alter their lifestyle or their surroundings.
[3]See Graciela Chichilnisky, *The Knowledge Revolution*, 7 J. OF INTERN. TRADE & ECONOMIC DEVELOPMENT 39-45 (1998) [A new pattern of economic growth – knowledge intensive growth – replaces the resource intensive patterns that prevailed hitherto].
[4]See CHARLES MORE, UNDERSTANDING THE INDUSTRIAL REVOLUTION (2000).

systems, and to constitutions, which cannot lightly be underestimated.[5] But as yet we are unsure of the economic, social, and legal effects of this technology.

There are however a number of reasons why the present high technology revolution is of crucial importance to governments. Some facets of the revolution[6] offer opportunities for internationalisation – or globalisation[7] – on a scale previously unimaginable.[8] Globalisation[9] is not merely a notion; it is an economic fact.[10] This is particularly so in the economic sphere, as legal systems are still (despite increasing cross-jurisdictional ties[11]) largely separate and distinct, the products of the sovereign state.[12] As Zekos has written, the real jurisdictional novelty of cyberspace[13] (which is perhaps the most frequently considered aspect of the

---

[5]See, for an ecological perspective, L. Ali Khan, THE EXTINCTION OF NATION-STATES: A WORLD WITHOUT BORDERS, 1 (1996).

[6]Particularly the Internet, and the telecommunications revolution in general; See Michael Leventhal, *The Golden Age of Wireless*, 14(1) INTELLECTUAL PROPERTY & TECHN. L. J. 1 (2002).

[7]For some of the effects of this, see MASATSUGU TSUJI, *Transformation of the Japanese system towards a network economy*, in EMANUELE GIOVANNETTI, MITSUHIRO KAGAMI & MASATSUGU TSUJI (eds), THE INTERNET REVOLUTION: A GLOBAL PERSPECTIVE (2003); Ian Tunstall, TAXATION AND THE INTERNET (2003); BRIAN KAHIN & CHARLES NESSON (eds), BORDERS IN CYBERSPACE: INFORMATION POLICY AND THE GLOBAL INFORMATION INFRASTRUCTURE (1997); Adam Czarnota, A few reflections on globalisation and the constitution of society, 24 U. NEW SOUTH WALES L. J. 809-816 (2001).

[8]Location remains important, but it is virtual location, rather than physical location – there is no necessary connection between an Internet address and a physical location.

[9]This might be defined as those processes which tend to create and consolidate a unified world economy, a single ecological system, and a complex network of communications that covers the whole globe, even if it does not penetrate every part of it; See WILLIAM TWINING, GLOBALISATION AND LEGAL THEORY 4-10 (1998).

[10]And it is also an extremely broad subject of study; Doron M. Kalir, Taking Globalisation Seriously: Towards General Jurisprudence, 39 COLUMBIA J. OF TRANSNATIONAL L. 785, 821 (2001).

[11]Particularly in international economic law.

[12]All law is prima facie territorial; American Banana Co v. United Fruit Co, 213 U.S. 347, 357 (1909).

[13]The term was coined by novelist William Gibson in 1984 to describe the boundless electronic system of interlinked networks of computers and

technological revolution), is that it will give rise to more frequent circumstances in which effects are felt in multiple territories at once.[14] This has implications for all states, and particularly so because it is an ongoing process,[15] whose eventual impact is unknown. At the same time the Internet provides states with tools through which they could potentially increase the level of control they exercise over their populations,[16] while also allowing individuals unparalleled access to information and commerce across the globe.[17] All of these effects have constitutional implications, or effects upon the very structure of government itself, both in their domestic and international aspects.

Technological advances in fields other than the Internet also challenge the boundaries of law, science, public policy, and ethics.[18] Biotechnology in general is highly controversial,[19] and particularly so is embryonic stem cell

---

bulletin boards that provided access to information and interactive communication; NEUROMANCER (1984). It is also referred to as the Internet, or the World Wide Web (www), whose architecture was designed by Sir Timothy Berners-Lee.

[14]Georgios Zekos, *Internet or Electronic Technology: A Threat to State Sovereignty*, 3 J. OF INFORM., L. & TECHN. (1999), available at <http://elj.warwick.ac.UK/jilt/99-3/zekos.html> (as at 28 November 2003).

[15]Doron M. Kalir, *Taking Globalisation Seriously: Towards General Jurisprudence*, 39 COLUMBIA J. OF TRANSNATIONAL L. 785, 802 (2001).

[16]"Big Brother" could very well be watching, given the increasing use of video surveillance cameras to combat crime in city streets, and the advent of effective face recognition software; From GEORGE ORWELL, NINETEEN EIGHTY-FOUR, A NOVEL (1949), the ubiquitous face of the party leader.

[17]See also WALTER B. WRISTON, THE TWILIGHT OF SOVEREIGNTY: HOW THE INFORMATION REVOLUTION IS TRANSFORMING OUR WORLD (1992) [examining the challenges to sovereignty posed by the information revolution].

[18]See Christine C. Vito, *State biotechnology oversight: the juncture of technology, law, and public policy*, 45 MAINE L. REV. 329-383 (1993); Organisation for Economic Co-operation and Development, BIO TECHNOLOGY AND THE CHANGING ROLE OF GOVERNMENT (1988); ROBERT H. BLANK, THE POLITICAL IMPLICATIONS OF HUMAN GENETIC TECHNOLOGY (1981); E. Donald Elliott, *The Genome and the law: Should increased genetic knowledge change the law?*, 25 HARV. J. OF L. & PUBL. POLICY 61 (2001).

[19]The mapping of the human genome allows doctors to screen out embryos with a genetic predilection for Alzheimer's disease. Genetic engineering may permit scientists to alter the genes of embryos and negate predilections

research.[20] Important developments are also occurring in artificial intelligence,[21] nano-technology,[22] and cryonics.[23] All of these raise legal and moral, if not constitutional questions. In an age where technological and medical advances are developing at what sometimes appears to be exponential rates, the law may shape or follow advances.[24] Each nation's scientific community must wait for approval, guidance, or funding to continue genetic research.[25] But it is not clear whether the state should follow or lead these developments.[26] In large part this is because although we speak of a revolution, in reality there are a number of interrelated changes, each of which must be considered – to some degree at least – as

---

for certain illnesses; See Kathy Hudson, *The Human Genome Project, DNA Science and the Law: the American Legal System's Response to Breakthroughs in Genetic Science*, 51 AM. UNIV. L. REV. 431 (2002); Cass R. Sunstein, *Keeping Up with the Cloneses*, 1 May 2002, THE NEW REPUBLIC ONLINE at <http://www.tnr.com/doc.mhtml?i=20020506&s=sunstein050602&c=1> (as at 9 December 2003); GREGORY STOCK, REDESIGNING HUMANS, OUR INEVITABLE GENETIC FUTURE (2002); LEE M. SILVER, REMAKING EDEN: HOW GENETIC ENGINEERING AND CLONING WILL TRANSFORM THE AMERICAN FAMILY, 266 (1998).

[20]See Denise Stevens, *Embryonic stem cell research: will President Bush's limitation on federal funding put the United States at a disadvantage? A comparison between U.S. and international law*, 25 HOUSTON J. OF INTERN. L. 623 (2003).

[21]See John McCarthy, *What is Artificial Intelligence?*, at <http://www-formal.stanford.edu/jmc/whatisai/whatisai.html> (as at 9 December 2003); Ulrich Furbach, *Principles of Artificial Intelligence*, 145 ARTIFICIAL INTELLIGENCE 245 (2003).

[22]See Glenn Harlan Reynolds, *Environmental Regulation of Nanotechnology: Some Preliminary Observations*, 31 ENVIRONMENTAL L. R. 10681 (2001).

[23]See Michael Janofsky, *Even for the Last .400 Hitter, Cryonics is the Longest Shot*, 10 July 2002 available at <http://www.nytimes.com/2002/07/10/science/10WILL.html?> (as at 9 December 2003).

[24]See James E. Bowman, *Symposium Genetics and the Law: the Ethical, Legal and Social Implications of Genetic Technology and Biomedical Ethics: The Road to Eugenics*, 3 U. CHICAGO L. SCH. ROUNDTABLE 491, 495-96, 501 (1996); Herbert Hovenkamp, *Technology, politics, and regulated monopoly: an American historical perspective*, 62 TEXAS L. REV. 1263-1312 (1984).

[25]See Charles F. De Jager, *The Development of Regulatory Standards for Gene Therapy in the European Union*, 18 FORDHAM INTERN. L. J. 1303, 1304, 1305 (1995).

[26]See Helen Szoke, *The nanny state or responsible government*, 227 J. OF L. & MEDICINE S-1 (2002).

separate. There have been warnings that decisions with respect to government involvement in high technology industries should be on a case-by-case basis and not of a general nature.[27] Indeed it has not been possible to avoid this. For law, this means a piecemeal approach to reform, and for the constitution[28] – where this is effected – potentially a lack of the coherency and consistency which should be the hallmark of a good constitution.[29]

Law cannot however be silent, whether at the constitutional level, or with respect to what may be called ordinary legislation.[30] There are risks inherent in any new technology. Sometimes there are errors – though these do not necessarily have to involve the very latest technology to have devastating consequences for communities.[31] It is particularly important in respect of technology transfer.[32] To leave all to chance may well however be

---

[27]See Genevieve Kirkwood & Michael Purdue, *High technology; role and status of central government policy*, J. OF PLANNING & ENVIRONMENTAL L. 111-118 (1988).

[28]The point must be here made that the term "constitutions" is not to be taken to refer to the formal written constitutional documents of a country, but rather to include all aspects of its governance, including the states underlying relationship with its people. It is not confined to the narrower modern definition of a constitution, such as exemplified by Lassalle (the written constitution of the modern state collects together and determines "in one instrument, on one piece of paper, all the country's institutions and principles of government" (2 Ferdinand Lassalle, "Uber Verfassungswesen" in E. BERNSTEIN (ed), GESAMMELTE REDEN UND SCHRIFTEN 38, 46 (1919)), but rather than more ancient and open definition, namely of a characteristic power structure and a minimal amount of legal norms about the structure of power; Hermann Heller, *The Decline of the Nation State and its Effect on Constitutional and International Economic Law*, 18 CARDOZO L. REV. 1139, 1206 (1996).

[29]It has been suggested by Scheuerman that we should see constitutions as expressive of a broadly-defined set of abstract moral principles; William E. Scheuerman, *Constitutionalism in an age of speed*, 19 CONSTITUTIONAL COMMENTARY 353, 366 (2002).

[30]That is, those dealing with specific technical details, and not the structure of the state or fundamental rights and responsibilities.

[31]See Shelly P. Battra, Robert E. Lutz, Ved P. Nanda, David A. Wirth, Daniel Magraw & Gunther Handl, *International transfer of hazardous technology and substances: caveat emptor or state responsibility? The case of Bhopal, India*, PROC. OF THE 79TH ANNUAL MEETING OF THE AM. SOC. OF INTERN. L. 303-322 (1985).

[32]See A.E SAFARIAN & GILLES Y. BERTIN (eds), MULTINATIONALS,

dangerous. In some cases governments have chosen to act, in others they have chosen to not do so. There have been debates – which have raged now for more than a decade – over whether the Internet is unique and should be governed (if regulated at all) by a sui generis "cyberlaw",[33] or is simply an extension of existing technology and can be regulated by existing laws. But it may well be asked how there can be agreement on a common approach, when laws, and public policy in general, are the product of the nation-state, and agreements between them is often difficult to achieve, even if it is desirable.

Fundamentally, this revolution raises questions about the role of state and society, and the place of the individual, and the state, within this structure, as well as the relationship between state and state. Modern state institutions, and the principal western models of state structures themselves,[34] were established or consolidated during the fifteenth to early twentieth century era of nation-state building.[35] That time also was a revolutionary one in its own way, which saw the decline of the Middle Ages and the growth of the modern era – and much of that political and legal change can be seen as grounded on technological change.[36] The present revolution raises questions about the nature of the state, just as earlier revolutions have done.

Weber's *The Protestant Ethic and the Spirit of Capitalism*[37] has been described as "a polemic that links the Protestant Revolution (the Reformation) and the Industrial Revolution, in particular, Calvinism and the rise of entrepreneurial capitalism."[38] McGready claims that the advent of

---

GOVERNMENTS, AND INTERNATIONAL TECHNOLOGY TRANSFER (1987).

[33]See Jack L. Goldsmith & Lawrence Lessig, *Grounding the Virtual Magistrate*, at <http://www.lessig.org/content/articles/works/magistrate.html> (as at 28 November 2003).

[34]At least those of the European model.

[35]Philip Cooke, *Globalisation of economic organisation and the emergence of regional interstate partnerships*, in Colin H. Williams (ed), THE POLITICAL GEOGRAPHY OF THE NEW WORLD ORDER 46-58, 47 (1993).

[36]See Steven McGready, *The Digital Reformation: Total Freedom, Risk, and Responsibility*, 10 HARV. J. OF L. & TECHN. 137 (1996).

[37]MAX WEBER, THE PROTESTANT ETHIC AND THE SPIRIT OF CAPITALISM, trans Talcott Parsons (1992).

[38]Steven McGready, *The Digital Reformation: Total Freedom, Risk, and Responsibility*, 10 HARV. J. OF L. & TECHN. 137, 138 (1996). Even those theorists who dispute Harvey's Marxist accounts of the origins of social and economic accelleration generally accept his observation that "the history of capitalism has been characterised by a speed-up in the pace of life"; David Harvey, THE CONDITION OF POSTMODERNITY 240 (1989).

the personal computer (PC) and the Internet is causing a reformation rather than a revolution.[39] A revolution changes political systems and governments; the Reformation changed almost every aspect of western European society, including religion, government, scholarship, education, and business.[40] He argues that the changes being wrought by the knowledge revolution will be as far-reaching as those of the Reformation.[41] Whilst this view is not necessarily shared by all, it is worth considering carefully.

One reason for this profound change, according to McGready, is that the new rights which aim to respond to opportunities and risks arising from new information and communication technologies, biotechnological or other technology-based industrial development, are not grounded in the nation-state. Generally, established civil, economic, social and political rights,[42] were predicated upon the existence of the nation-state, and indeed were constructed within the framework of the nation-state.[43] Globalisation, and a concurrent individualisation (or the enfranchisement of the individual) has led to additional rights, desires and pressures.[44] But the state is not unassailable.[45] The state's potential loss of power and autonomy to regulate economic and social activity, as well as to protect individual rights, has been accepted in the European Union as a result of a process that to a certain degree anticipated contemporary global tendencies,[46] but which is so

---

[39]Steven McGready, *The Digital Reformation: Total Freedom, Risk, and Responsibility*, 10 HARV. J. OF L. & TECHN. 137, 139 (1996).

[40]See NORMAN JONES, THE ENGLISH REFORMATION: RELIGION AND CULTURAL ADAPTATION (2002); ETHAN H. SHAGAN, POPULAR POLITICS AND THE ENGLISH REFORMATION (2003); ELMORE HERBISON, THE CHRISTIAN SCHOLAR IN THE AGE OF THE REFORMATION (1956); LEWIS W. SPITZ, THE REFORMATION: EDUCATION AND HISTORY (1997); and JOSEPH LOEWENSTEIN, THE AUTHOR'S DUE: PRINTING AND THE PREHISTORY OF COPYRIGHT (2002) respectively.

[41]See Steven McGready, *The Digital Reformation: Total Freedom, Risk, and Responsibility*, 10 HARV. J. OF L. & TECHN. 137 (1996).

[42]See, for instance, the Universal Declaration of Human Rights, as passed and proclaimed by the General Assembly of the United Nations on the tenth day of December 1948 (1951).

[43]See Maria Eduarda Goncalves, *Technological change, globalisation and the Europeanisation of rights*, 16 INTERN. REV. OF L., COMPUTERS & TECHN. 301-316 (2002).

[44]Such as raised economic and political expectations in poorer and less democratic countries.

[45]See Martin Wolf, *Will the nation-state survive globalisation?*, 80(1) FOREIGN AFFAIRS 178-190 (2001).

[46]See Maria Eduarda Goncalves, *Technological change, globalisation and the*

far the best example of a modern multi-national quasi-state.

In 1996 Khan argued that the evolution of a world without borders seemed unavoidable.[47] He postulated a theory of a Free State, relying on Hugo Grotius, most particularly *The Law of War and Peace*.[48] Yet it is possibly premature to consign the nation-state to the rubbish bin of history,[49] not least because, despite continued falls in the costs of transport and communications in the first half of the twentieth century, integration actually reversed course – for predominantly political reasons.[50] But it may well be necessary to re-examine the place of the state in the new world technological order.[51]

Europeanisation of rights, 16 INTERN. REV. OF L. COMPUTERS & TECHN. 301-316 (2002).

[47]L. ALI KHAN, THE EXTINCTION OF NATION-STATES: A WORLD WITHOUT BORDERS, 1 (1996).

[48]DE JURE BELLI AC PACIS ed F.W. Kelsey (1964).

[49]Wolf, for instance, argues that the nation-state is not endangered by globalisation. His reasons are that the ability of a society to take advantage of the opportunities offered by international economic integration depends on the quality of public goods; the state normally defines identity; and International governance rests on the ability of individual states to provide and guarantee stability; Martin Wolf, *Will the nation-state survive globalisation?*, 80 FOREIGN AFFAIRS 178-190 (2001).

[50]See Martin Wolf, *Will the nation-state survive globalisation?*, 80 FOREIGN AFFAIRS 178-190 (2001).

[51]The term "new world order" has been much used in the context of the global security system, but it arguably has greater relevance in the economic sphere, where it is more clearly developing. See Laura Yavitz, *The WTO and the environment: the Shrimp case that created a new world*, 16 J. OF NATURAL RESOURCES & ENVIRONMENTAL L. 203-255 (2001), cf Ernest Easterly, III, *The rule of law and the new world order*, 22 SOUTHERN UNIV. L. REV. 161-183 (1995).

Cortada examines the historical, cultural, and (to some degree) legal aspects of interaction between society and information.[52] He maintains that the information age is not really a new phenomenon, but rather is the most recent manifestation of a long-standing process of historical evolution.[53] Yet Lessig suggests that the historical evolution of the information society is a foundational preamble for what he characterises as one of the most critical battles of our time – the battle for the future of the Internet.[54] Both views may be correct, for while the knowledge technology may be grounded in an earlier Industrial Revolution, so evolution has it periods of stagnation, and its periods of fundamental change.[55] We may be entering just such a latter phase now.

The challenge for governments is to respond to this ongoing – and possibly long-term[56] – revolution,[57] and not become victims of it.[58] The more inflexible the state – or the more dogmatic – the greater the risk of failure.[59] Failure by governments to respond fully and effectively to changing paradigms[60] can result in loss of competitive advantage[61] – or even

---

[52]See JAMES W. CORTADA, MAKING THE INFORMATION SOCIETY: EXPERIENCE, CONSEQUENCES AND POSSIBILITIES (2001).

[53]See JAMES W. CORTADA, MAKING THE INFORMATION SOCIETY: EXPERIENCE, CONSEQUENCES AND POSSIBILITIES (2001).

[54]See LAWRENCE LESSIG, THE FUTURE OF IDEAS: THE FATE OF THE COMMONS IN A CONNECTED WORLD (2001).

[55]See later sections.

[56]It is, of course, impossible to predict what further developments are likely to occur, which makes it necessary that the legal system – and the constitution – is sufficiently flexible so as to allow this development, and yet restrict or prohibit developments which are deemed unsuitable.

[57]See Ilene K. Grossman, *The new Industrial Revolution: meeting the challenge*, 4 PUBL. L. FORUM 419-426 (1985); Thomas W. Rudin, *State involvement in the 'new Industrial Revolution'*, 4 PUBL. L. FORUM 411-417 (1985).

[58]See MAURICE PEARTON, THE KNOWLEDGE STATE: DIPLOMACY, WAR, AND TECHNOLOGY SINCE 1830 (1982).

[59]See Bruce Parrott, *Technology and the Soviet polity: the problem of industrial innovation, 1928 to 1973*, COLUMBIA UNIV. PHD THESIS (1976); Rensselaer W. Lee, *The politics of technology in Communist China*, STANFORD UNIV. PHD THESIS (1973).

[60]A paradigmatic is a technical concept derived from linguistics and semiotics, used in anthropological theories of meaning, to denote the stable, rule-governed aspect of communication (opposite of syntagmatic, that which flows and moves in time). The concept is often used more loosely about basic premises underlying communication (as grammar underlies language). "Paradigmatic shifts" should thus be understood as fundamental

the existence of that state (though loss of economic viability).[62] This ability to respond is not merely political, social or economic. It is also constitutional. Fundamentally, the challenge – or threat – of techno-globalism to sovereign states[63] has profound implications for jurisprudence.[64]

This work is not concerned with the laws governing the Internet, or genetic engineering, or of the knowledge revolution per se.[65] It is not concerned with the social or economic implications of these revolutions – profound though they may be.[66] It is concerned with the effect of technological change upon the structure of government – upon the constitution – and, to a lesser extent, how the structure of governments

---

changes in the premises of communication; THOMAS KUHN, THE STRUCTURE OF SCIENTIFIC REVOLUTIONS (1962) [a discussion of revolutionary change in the system of scientific knowledge production].

[61]For example, see HOUSE OF REPRESENTATIVES STANDING COMMITTEE FOR LONG TERM STRATEGIES, GOVERNMENT RESPONSE: AUSTRALIA AS AN INFORMATION SOCIETY: GRASPING NEW PARADIGMS (1992); NICK MOORE & JANE STEELE, INFORMATION-INTENSIVE BRITAIN: AN ANALYSIS OF THE POLICY ISSUES (1991), where the emphasis of both is upon information technology. See also JAMES BOTKIN, DAN DIMANCESCU, RAY STATA & JOHN MCCLELLAN, GLOBAL STAKES: THE FUTURE OF HIGH TECHNOLOGY IN AMERICA (1982); THOMAS L. FRIEDMAN, THE LEXUS AND THE OLIVE TREE, 9 (2000).

[62]Response does not mean single-issue responses, but refers rather to the matching of constitution and society.

[63]See SYLVIA OSTRY & RICHARD R. NELSON, TECHNO-NATIONALISM AND TECHNO-GLOBALISM: CONFLICT AND COOPERATION (1995).

[64]See CATHERINE DAUVERGNE (ed), JURISPRUDENCE FOR AN INTERCONNECTED GLOBE (2003); RICHARD WARREN PERRY & BILL MAURER (eds), GLOBALISATION UNDER CONSTRUCTION: GOVERNMENTALITY, LAW, AND IDENTITY (2003); Jean Stefancic & Richard Delgado, *Outsider jurisprudence and the electronic revolution: Will technology help or hinder the cause of law reform?*, 52 OHIO ST. L. J. 847-858 (1991).

[65]For each of which there is an ample literature.

[66]For a discussion of the nexus between social change and the law, see ALAN WATSON, SOCIETY AND LEGAL CHANGE (2d ed. 2001). It has also been observed that recent finance scholarship finds that countries with legal systems based on the common law have more developed financial markets than civil-law countries; See Robert G. King & Ross Levine, *Finance and Growth: Schumpeter Might Be Right*, 108 QUARTERLY J. OF ECONOMICS 717 (1993). This may be due to the common law's association with limited government; Paul G. Mahoney, *The Common Law and Economic Growth: Hayek might be right*, 30 J. OF LEGAL STUDIES 503 (2001).

may in turn have effected technological changes.[67] In effect it is an attempt to identify a link between the societal and economic effects of technology, and the societal and economic influences technology has on constitutions. It is primarily from a constitutional rather than a technological perspective that this issue is approached. From this we may obtain some guidance as to how constitutions might best respond to technological change, and how they might be restructured to best facilitate that change in a way which is for the long-term good.

The work begins with a brief examination of the nature of constitutions, and of their relationship with society and technology. It will then proceed to briefly examine several seminal technological eras or changes in the past, in an attempt to identify the effect that these may have had upon government, and the ways in which they were influenced in their development by the nature and form of government. It will then look at several contemporary technological revolutions, with a similar purpose. Finally, it will seek to draw some common themes from these examples, with the intention of identifying some lessons to guide law and policy-makers.

The nature of constitutions and their relationships with technology

The scope of this work is the effect of changes in technology upon governments – more particularly, upon constitutions. This is partly an historical analysis. The reason for this is that law, as a human artefact, is inseparable from history.[68] Constitutional laws – those which are concerned with the structure and powers of states – are also the product of history.[69]

---

[67]There is a considerable body of work on the nexus between constitutions and social and economic change; from the U.S. perspective, for example, see JOHN R. VILE, THE CONSTITUTIONAL AMENDING PROCESS IN AMERICAN POLITICAL THOUGHT, 137-156 (1992); DANIEL LAZARE, THE FROZEN REPUBLIC: HOW THE CONSTITUTION IS PARALYSING DEMOCRACY (1996); DAVID E. KYVIG, EXPLICIT AND AUTHENTIC ACTS: AMENDING THE U.S. CONSTITUTION 216-314 (1996); Richard Kay, Constitutional Chrononomy, 13 RATIO JURIS 31, 33 (2000).

[68]L. ALI KHAN, THE EXTINCTION OF NATION-STATES: A WORLD WITHOUT BORDERS, 1 (1996).

[69]Indeed, a constitutional lawyer must be as much an historian (and political scientist) as he or she is a lawyer, and the reverse holds true also; See Noel Cox, *The Evolution of the New Zealand Monarchy: The Recognition of an Autochthonous Polity*, U. AUCKLAND PHD THESIS (2001).

Indeed, they may be more strictly linked to history than other laws, because of their need for legitimacy, which is derived in part from continuity and acquiescence.[70] But these laws are also influenced by technology,[71] and by economics,[72] as well as by societal change.

With the dominance of democratic concepts of government,[73] it might be thought that if the people believe that a governmental institution is appropriate, then it is legitimate.[74] But this scheme leaves out substantive questions about the justice of the state and the protection it offers the individuals who belong to it.[75] It is generally more usual to maintain that a

---

[70]Amongst modern states this is nowhere more apparently than in the U.K., where, until recently, many of its political institutions dated from mediæval times; See *The Survival of Mediæval Institutions*, in A.H. Birch, THE BRITISH SYSTEM OF GOVERNMENT (4th ed. 1980).

[71]See Tom W. Bell, *Free speech, strict scrutiny, and self-help: how technology upgrades constitutional jurisprudence*, 87 MINNESOTA L. REV. 743-778 (2003); Mark S. Kende, *Technology's future impact upon state constitutional law: the Montana example*, 64 MONTANA L. REV. 273-294 (2003); Deborah Jones Merritt, *The Constitution in a brave new world: a century of technological change and constitutional law*, 69 OREGON L. REV. 1-45 (1990).

[72]Only systematic empirical research can demonstrate whether social and economic accelleration actually contributes to the amplification of the executive authority long observed by political scientists and legal scholars; William E. Scheuerman, *Constitutionalism in an age of speed*, 19 CONSTITUTIONAL COMMENTARY 353 (2002), 385-386. The reverse may well happen also. The late Saxon legal and fiscal system was comparatively sophisticated, and its efficiency was one of the principal reasons for the strength of the Norman kingdom which was to follow; Noel Cox, *The Influence of the Common Law and the Decline of the Ecclesiastical Courts of the Church of England*, 3 RUTGERS J. OF L. & RELIGION 1-45 (2001-2002) at <http://www-camlaw.rutgers.edu/publications/law-religion/Cox1.PDF> n 19 (as at 28 November 2003).

[73]Initially in western liberal democracies, and by extension, particularly through such institutions as the Commonwealth, throughout most of the world; *The Harare Commonwealth Declaration, 1991,* issued by Heads of Government in Harare, Zimbabwe, 20 October 1991, available at <http://www.thecommonwealth.org/gender/htm/commonwealth/about/declares/harare.htm> (as at 6 December 2003).

[74]Penelope Brook Cowen, *Neo Liberalism*, in RAYMOND MILLER (ed), NEW ZEALAND POLITICS IN TRANSITION, 341 (1997).

[75]This is illustrated by the study of the application of the model to Mummar Qadhafi's Libya; Saleh Al Namlah, *Political legitimacy in Libya since 1969*, SYRACUSE UNIV. PHD THESIS (1992).

state's legitimacy depends upon its upholding certain human rights.[76] But the state is as much an economic as it is a social construct,[77] and it is important for its legitimacy and viability that the constitution remains broadly consistent with economic, and technological, realities.

Economic and technological changes eventually alter constitutions, because they change society, which constitutions reflect to a greater or lesser degree.[78] Constitutional reform itself may be revolutionary, yet maintain continuity.[79] Changes need not be revolutionary in a legal sense. Indeed, the formalist approach of Kelsen maintains that if the constitution is changed according to its own provisions, then the state and its legal order remain the same.[80] In this view it does not matter how fundamental changes in the substance of the legal norms may be; if they are performed in conformity with the provisions of the constitution, continuity of the legal system will not be interrupted.[81] Thus, even though the nature of the relationship between individual and state – or between state and state – may have been profoundly altered, there is no revolutionary change to the constitution.[82]

Ross on the other hand emphasises the necessary discontinuity of a new constitutional order which has replaced an earlier one.[83] According to Ross, the legitimacy of a constitutional order goes beyond the legal system. If the political ideology changes at a time of constitutional change, so the legal continuity is disrupted.[84] In other words, if technology – or any other

---

[76]See JOHN RAWLS, POLITICAL LIBERALISM (1993); TED HONDERICH (ed), THE OXFORD COMPANION TO PHILOSOPHY, 477 (1995); Matthew Swanson, *The social extract tradition and the question of political legitimacy*, U. MISSOURI-COLUMBIA PHD THESIS (1995).

[77]See, for instance, JOHN LOCKE; MARTYN P. THOMPSON, IDEAS OF CONTRACT IN ENGLISH POLITICAL THOUGHT IN THE AGE OF JOHN LOCKE (1987).

[78]See, generally, J. Woodford Howard Jr, *Constitution and society in comparative perspective*, 71 JUDICATURE 211-215 (1987).

[79]See Peter Paczolay, *Constitutional Transition and Legal Continuity*, 8 CONNECTICUT J. OF INTERN. L. 559 (1993); Ralf Dahrendorf, *Transitions: Politics, Economics, and Liberty*, 13 WASHINGTON QUARTERLY 134 (1990).

[80]HANS KELSEN, GENERAL THEORY OF LAW AND STATE, trans Anders Wedberg 117-118 (1945).

[81]HANS KELSEN, GENERAL THEORY OF LAW AND STATE, trans Anders Wedberg 119 (1945).

[82]And therefore the knowledge revolution would be economic and social, but not political.

[83]See ALF ROSS, ON LAW AND JUSTICE (1958).

[84]See ALF ROSS, ON LAW AND JUSTICE (1958).

influence – has resulted in a profound social, political, or economic change, any resulting constitutional change may well be revolutionary in nature.[85]

But if we wish to understand the relationship between constitution and technology, it is also important to consider the purpose of the state – though this has been a fundamental problem of all theories of the state since Aristotle.[86] Grady and McGuire have considered the nature of constitutions from an economic perspective. They have concluded that constitutions are not a product of consensual choice, but rather the result of weaker humans banding together to resist forceful appropriations from more dominant humans.[87] This may fit one economic model, but it does not necessarily assist us greatly when we consider the constitutional implications of the knowledge revolution. This revolutionary potential involves the empowerment of smaller and smaller groups, until one reaches the nadir, the wholly empowered individual. It is possibly true that no true Lockean constitution (where state and society are in a true compact[88]) exists today.[89] However consent – through acquiescence and participation – is found in most governmental systems.[90]

Let us begin with a review of four theories of the origin of the state, courtesy of Grady and McGuire.[91] These theories are the Hobbes-Buchanan contractarian theory, Karl Wittfogel's hydraulic despotism theory, Robert Carneiro's circumscription theory, and Mancur Olson's stationary bandit theory.[92]

---

[85]See, for instance, F.M. BROOKFIELD, WAITANGI AND INDIGENOUS RIGHTS: REVOLUTION, LAW, AND LEGITIMATION (1999) (revolutionary seizure of power through legal means).

[86]He maintained that:

Πασα κοινονια αγατηου τιϖοσ ηενεκα συνεστεκεν

("All associations are instituted for the purpose of attaining some good").

– THE POLITICS OF ARISTOTLE, trans Ernest Barker, 1 (1958), cited by Hermann Heller, *The Decline of the Nation State and its Effect on Constitutional and International Economic Law*, 18 CARDOZO L. REV. 1139 (1996).

[87]See Mark F. Grady & Michael T. McGuire, *The Nature of Constitutions*, 1 J. OF BIOECONOMICS 227 (1999).

[88]See MARTYN P. THOMPSON, IDEAS OF CONTRACT IN ENGLISH POLITICAL THOUGHT IN THE AGE OF JOHN LOCKE (1987).

[89]If it ever did.

[90]See Noel Cox, "The Evolution of the New Zealand Monarchy: The Recognition of an Autochthonous Polity" (2001) University of Auckland PhD thesis, chapter 2.

[91]See Mark F. Grady & Michael T. McGuire, *The Nature of Constitutions*, 1 J. OF BIOECONOMICS 227 (1999).

[92]THOMAS HOBBES, LEVIATHAN, ed Edwin Curley (1994); James

Thomas Hobbes famously began his analysis with a consideration of the state of nature. He assumed that before formal governments existed people were reasonably equal in endowments.[93] From this rough equality of mental and physical assets, each had an equal hope of acquiring the same ends, which were scarce. Each depended for his or her livelihood on their own efforts, and those of their family.[94] As a consequence, individuals fell into competition with each other, which resulted in the "war of every man against every man."[95] In such a state, opportunities for production, investment, learning, and exchange were limited, because each individual possessed "continual fear and danger of violent death."[96] Life was, or could very easily be, "nasty, brutish and short."[97] In order to relieve themselves of eternal conflict, individuals have an incentive to organise themselves into a commonwealth, which is a hierarchy that "tie[s] them by fear of punishment to the performance of their covenants and observation of th[e] laws of nature .... "[98] They institute this commonwealth by giving a

---

Buchanan, THE LIMITS OF LIBERTY: BETWEEN ANARCHY AND LEVIATHAN (1975); KARL A. WITTFOGEL, ORIENTAL DESPOTISM: A COMPARATIVE STUDY OF TOTAL POWER (1957); Robert L. Carneiro, *A Theory of the Origin of the State*, 169 SCIENCE 733 (1970); Mancur Olson, *Dictatorship, Democracy, and Development*, 87 AM. POLI. SCI. REV. 567 (1993).
[93]He wrote:

Nature hath made men so equal in the faculties of body and mind as that, though there be found one man sometimes manifestly stronger in body or of quicker mind than another, yet when all is reckoned together the difference between man and man is not so considerable as that one man can thereupon claim to himself any benefit to which another may not pretend as well as he.

– THOMAS HOBBES, LEVIATHAN, ed Edwin Curley, 74 (1994).
[94]See J. DESMOND CLARK, THE COMMON HERITAGE: THE SIGNIFICANCE OF HUNTER-GATHERER SOCIETIES FOR HUMAN EVOLUTION (1990).
[95]Thomas Hobbes, LEVIATHAN, ed Edwin Curley, 76 (1994). For Hobbes, war did not consist only of actual battles, but also threats of battle ("For War consisteth not in battle only, or the act of fighting, but in a tract of time wherein the will to contend by battle is sufficiently known").
[96]THOMAS HOBBES, LEVIATHAN, ed Edwin Curley, 76 (1994).
[97]"No arts; no letters; no society; and which is worst of all, continual fear and danger of violent death; and the life of man, solitary, poor, nasty, brutish, and short"; THOMAS HOBBES, LEVIATHAN, ed Edwin Curley, Part i. Chap. xviii (1994).
[98]THOMAS HOBBES, LEVIATHAN, ed Edwin Curley, 106 (1994).

monarch or an assembly the right to represent them.[99] Government, then, was a product of consensual alliance, and whilst it was generally for the common good, its primary purpose was to further the interests of the individual.[100]

The new social and political structures potentially facilitated by information technology offer the possibility of something very much like a constitutional contract,[101] though not necessarily with existing states or forms of states.[102] Existing states may be much more complex constitutional structures than the Hobbesian constitution would appear to suggest.

In Grady and McGuire's view,[103] Hobbes and Buchanan[104] have not fully addressed the problem of sovereign appropriation. At least Hobbes assumed that the sovereign would behave benevolently. Nevertheless, with a monopoly of force over a particular geographic area, a sovereign possesses a private incentive to appropriate from his or her subjects.[105] This

---

[99]THOMAS HOBBES, LEVIATHAN, ed Edwin Curley, 110 (1994).

[100]See, generally, works on sixteenth and seventeenth century political economy; GERALD AYLMER, THE STRUGGLE FOR THE CONSTITUTION, 1603-1689: ENGLAND IN THE SEVENTEENTH CENTURY (4th ed. 1975); JOHN POCOCK, THE ANCIENT CONSTITUTION AND THE FEUDAL LAW: A STUDY OF ENGLISH HISTORICAL THOUGHT IN THE SEVENTEENTH CENTURY (1987).

[101]For an example, see RONALD M. PETERS, JR., THE MASSACHUSETTS CONSTITUTION OF 1780: A SOCIAL COMPACT (1978).

[102]See, for instance, the arguments of the "cyberspace"; John Perry Barlow, co-founder of the Electronic Frontier Foundation (EFF), made the seminal statement to this effect:

Governments of the Industrial World, you weary giants of flesh and steel, I come from Cyberspace, the new home of the Mind. On behalf of the future, I ask you of the past to leave us alone. You are not welcome among us. You have no sovereignty where we gather.

– John Perry Barlow, *A Declaration of the Independence of Cyberspace*, <http://www.eff.org/pub/Publications/John_Perry_Barlow/barlow_0296 .declaration> (as at 6 December 2003).

[103]See Mark F. Grady & Michael T. McGuire, *The Nature of Constitutions*, 1 J. OF BIOECONOMICS 227 (1999).

[104]See JAMES BUCHANAN, THE LIMITS OF LIBERTY: BETWEEN ANARCHY AND LEVIATHAN (1975).

[105]See Mark F. Grady & Michael T. McGuire, *The Nature of Constitutions*, 1 J. OF BIOECONOMICS 227 (1999).

however is unlikely to happen because the ruler will wish to retain power. When over-reaching occurs, revolution will occasionally restore the balance.[106]

The networked economy,[107] by creating a greater mobility of people and assets, reduces the ability of sovereigns to appropriate because their subjects can more easily exit over-reaching regimes.[108] The reduction in transaction costs created by the Internet and by information technology more generally creates the possibility of competing Hobbesian commonwealths, each constituted by customers and dependent upon their continuing loyalty. This view was widely held in the halcyon days of Internet growth in the 1990s[109] – but has since fallen out of favour.[110] But, whilst the Hobbesian state was a social construct, it would appear that its nature – even its existence – was determined by the technological limitations of its makers. If this is so (and this work will proceed to consider the effect of technology on constitutions), fundamental changes in technology may – and perhaps should – result in changes to the

---

[106]Formerly great theologians of the Church like St Thomas Aquinas [SUMMA THEOLOGICA, ed John A. Oesterle, II-II, Q. xlii, a.2 (1964)], Francisco Suarez [*Defensio fidei*, book VI, ch iv, p 15, in SELECTIONS FROM THREE WORKS: DE LEGIBUS, AC DEO LEGISLATORS, 1612, DEFENSIO FIDEI CATHOLICAE, ET APOSTOLICAE ADVERSUS ANGLICANAE SECTAE ERRORES, 1613, DE TRIPLICI VIRTUTE THEOLOGICA, FIDE, SPE, ET CHARITATE, 1621, trans Gwladys L. Williams, Ammi Brown & John Waldron (1944)], and Domingo Bañez, O.P. [DE JUSTITIA ET JURE, Q. lxiv, a. 3], permitted rebellion against oppressive rulers when the tyranny had become extreme and when no other means of safety were available. This carried to its logical conclusion the doctrine of the Middle Ages that the supreme ruling authority comes from God through the people for the public good. As the people immediately give sovereignty to the ruler, so the people can deprive him of his sovereignty when he has used his power oppressively (mediæval rulers were seldom women).

[107]It has been said that a global economy is largely replacing and overwhelming national and regional economies; Louis Henkin, *That S. Words: Sovereignty, and Globalisation, and Human Rights, Et Cetera*, 68 FORD L. REV. 1, 5-6 (1999).

[108]See, for instance, Noel Cox, *Tax and regulatory avoidance through non-traditional alternatives to tax havens*, 9(3) NEW ZEALAND J. OF TAXATION L. & POLICY 305-327 (2003).

[109]See David R. Johnson & David G. Post, *Law and Borders: The Rise of Law in Cyberspace*, 48 STANFORD L. REV. 1367 (1996).

[110]See Jonathan B. Wolf, *War games meets the internet: Chasing 21st century cybercriminals with old laws and little money*, 28 AM. J. OF CRIMINAL LAW 95 (2000).

constitution itself. If the individual's need for protection, assistance, or supervision, is reduced (or disappears), so the role of the state changes.[111]

The second theory of the state we will consider is that of Karl Wittfogel. In his 1957 book *Oriental Despotism*,[112] Wittfogel argued that despotic governments often arose around rivers, as in ancient Egypt, China, and Mesopotamia. He theorised that the state arose when villages banded together to develop common irrigation projects, which vastly improved the productivity of agriculture.[113] Nevertheless, once the state came into being as a means of developing irrigation, it soon turned its bureaucracy to oppressive purposes.[114] In fact, according to Wittfogel, what he termed an hydraulic state will cease appropriating only when the marginal cost of further administrative control begins to exceed the marginal revenue to those benefiting from state action.[115] This is fundamentally a technology-

---

[111]The converse is true also. In the course of the Industrial Revolution the scale and complexity of the state grew enormously, in part as a consequence of the technological change, and as a result of the social changes which these wrought. See, for instance, Steven Puro, *Technology, politics and the new Industrial Revolution*, 4 PUBL. L. FORUM 387-398 (1985).

[112]See KARL A. WITTFOGEL, ORIENTAL DESPOTISM: A COMPARATIVE STUDY OF TOTAL POWER (1957).

[113]He wrote:

In a landscape characterised by full aridity permanent agriculture becomes possible only if and when coordinated human action transfers a plentiful and accessible water supply from its original location to a potentially fertile soil. When this is done, government-led hydraulic enterprise is identical with the creation of agricultural life. This first and crucial moment may therefore be designated as the "administrative creation point."

– KARL A. WITTFOGEL, ORIENTAL DESPOTISM: A COMPARATIVE STUDY OF TOTAL POWER, 109 (1957).

[114]KARL A. WITTFOGEL, ORIENTAL DESPOTISM: A COMPARATIVE STUDY OF TOTAL POWER, 126-136 (1957).

[115]Wittfogel wrote:

The power of the hydraulic despotism is unchecked ("total"), but it does not operate everywhere. The life of most individuals is far from being completely controlled by the state; and there are many villages and other corporate units that are not totally controlled either.

What keeps despotic power from asserting its authority in spheres of life? Modifying a key formula of classical economics, we may say that the

driven model of the state.[116]

In an influential article, the anthropologist Robert Carneiro theorised that states began in areas of environmental or social circumscription.[117] Carneiro looked at the places where states first arose, areas such as the Nile, Tigris-Euphrates, and Indus valleys in the Old World and the Valley of Mexico and the mountain and coastal valleys of Peru in the New World. He found that all were areas of "circumscribed agricultural land."[118] In his words, "[e]ach of them is set off by mountains, seas, or deserts, and these environmental features sharply delimit the area that simple farming peoples could occupy and cultivate."[119] He contrasted these "environmentally circumscribed" areas to areas in which states did not arise as early, for instance, the Amazon basin and the eastern woodlands of North America.[120] From this we might conclude that states arose when competition for scarce responses – with no room for expansion – reached a critical level. The necessity of economic survival led to the development of settled states.[121] This may be less obviously a technology-driven state. But even here it was the degree of technological development which determined when this critical level which led to state development would occur.[122] Settled

---

representatives of the hydraulic regime act (or refrain from acting) in response to the law of diminishing administrative returns.

– KARL A. WITTFOGEL, ORIENTAL DESPOTISM: A COMPARATIVE STUDY OF TOTAL POWER, 108-109 (1957). In Roman times whole districts were laid waste by the depredation of the tax collectors. See, generally, Jean Andreau, BANKING AND BUSINESS IN THE ROMAN WORLD trans Janet Lloyd (1999).

[116]Remembering the definition of technology as processes and things people create for the purpose of using them to alter their lifestyle or their surroundings.

[117]Robert L. Carneiro, *A Theory of the Origin of the State*, 169 SCIENCE 733, 738 (1970).

[118]Robert L. Carneiro, *A Theory of the Origin of the State*, 169 SCIENCE 733, 734 (1970). The degree of circumscription varied considerably.

[119]Robert L. Carneiro, *A Theory of the Origin of the State*, 169 SCIENCE 733, 734-735 (1970).

[120]Robert L. Carneiro, *A Theory of the Origin of the State*, 169 SCIENCE 733, 735 (1970). It might be countered that the Amazonian jungle provided a commensurate degree of circumscription – and even the woodlands of North America may have done so.

[121]See ANTHONY MOLHO, KURT RAAFLAUB & JULIA EMLEN, CITY STATES IN CLASSICAL ANTIQUITY AND MEDIEVAL ITALY (1991).

[122]The processes used to alter their lifestyles beng settled agriculture –

agriculture – as distinct from the hunter-gatherer culture – was a more technologically advanced economic structure,[123] which led to a more advanced constitution.

In the fourth and last of the models of the state considered by Grady and McGuire,[124] Mancur Olson has argued that the state can be likened to a stationary bandit who robs the people within his or her jurisdiction (through taxes and the like) and protects them from roving bandits.[125] Olson argues that ruled people prefer a stationary bandit to roving bandits because the stationary bandit has an incentive to invest in public goods that increase the people's wealth and therefore the tax revenues that can be extracted from them.[126] This theory is very similar to a more general theory developed independently by Grady and McGuire to explain primate, including human, political structures.[127]

The basic idea common to both Grady and McGuire's theory and Olson's is that the sovereign[128] is effectively the residual claimant of the group he or she rules.[129] When the group creates a surplus, the sovereign is in a position to appropriate that surplus. Olson stressed that the sovereign's position of residual claimant could induce the sovereign to create public goods, such as irrigation projects (to use Wittfogel's example); then, the sovereign could appropriate the surplus from these investments.[130] The sovereign would have a self-interested incentive to keep peace within the group and even to enforce efficient private law because these kinds of legal rules would increase the surplus from group activities and therefore create a

---

including animal husbandry.

[123]See MAX WEBER, THE AGRARIAN SOCIOLOGY OF ANCIENT CIVILISATIONS trans R.I. Frank (1976).

[124]See Mark F. Grady & Michael T. McGuire, *A Theory of the Origin of Natural Law*, 8 J. OF CONTEMPORARY LEGAL ISSUES 87 (1997).

[125]Mancur Olson, *Dictatorship, Democracy, and Development*, 87 AM. POLI. SCI. REV. 567, 568-570 (1993).

[126]Mancur Olson, *Dictatorship, Democracy, and Development*, 87 AM. POLI. SCI. REV. 567, 569 (1993).

[127]See Mark F. Grady & Michael T. McGuire, *A Theory of the Origin of Natural Law*, 8 J. OF CONTEMPORARY LEGAL ISSUES 87 (1997).

[128]Meaning the holder of authority in a state, not necessarily limited to hereditary monarchs of traditional form.

[129]The Crown, in British law and practice remains the residual landlord, and entitled to the assets of those who die without any heirs, under the doctrine of *bona vacantia*; Chris Ryan, "'The Crown' and corporate bona vacantia" (1982) 12(1) Kingston Law Review 75-87.

[130]Mancur Olson, *Dictatorship, Democracy, and Development*, 87 AM. POLI. SCI. REV. 567, 569-571 (1993).

greater possibility for sovereign appropriations.[131] The surplus, as in ancient Egypt, was then at the disposal of the state, which might use it to undertake further public works or to feed the population in times of need.[132] The 'surplus' model may be correct – but it was very often the existence of a technological system which enabled this surplus to be achieved.[133]

Technology does not change the essential problems that constitutions seek to address, because these have deeper root, being rooted in the enduring nature of humanity.[134] Not only can technology transform the human environment,[135] but a different environment may substantially modify the constitution. As Burke recognised, the key to sound structures of governance in every age and place is to understand the intersection of humanity's enduring nature with its particular circumstance.[136]

Just as the Reformation, and later the Industrial Revolution, opened up new economic opportunities – and resulted in significant constitutional changes – so the new globally networked economy greatly expands opportunities for exit from the sway of local monopoly, whether sovereign or private.[137] These new "commonwealths" operate on a radically different economic principle than traditional geographic empires or nation-states. Existing states may be seen as having developed from the Hobbesian model – based as they were on mutual interdependence. This interdependence remains – for no foreseeable technological innovation could make an individual entirely independent.[138] However, dependence is no longer

---

[131]See Mark F. Grady & Michael T. McGuire, *A Theory of the Origin of Natural Law*, 8 J. OF CONTEMPORARY LEGAL ISSUES 87, 118-120 (1997).

[132]For Egyptian administration generally, see KLAUS BAER, RANK AND TITLE IN THE OLD KINGDOM; THE STRUCTURE OF THE EGYPTIAN ADMINISTRATION IN THE FIFTH AND SIXTH DYNASTIES (1960); NAGUIB KANAWATI, THE EGYPTIAN ADMINISTRATION IN THE OLD KINGDOM: EVIDENCE ON ITS ECONOMIC DECLINE (1977). See also JOSEPH G. MANNING, LAND AND POWER IN PTOLEMAIC EGYPT: THE STRUCTURE OF LAND TENURE (2003).

[133]This may be governmental technology, or human resouce management, rather than mechanical technology (though even this latter played a part).

[134]See John O. McGinnis, *The Symbiosis of Constitutionalism and Technology*, 25 HARV. J. OF L. & PUBL. POLICY 3 (2001).

[135]Including economic and social environment.

[136]EDMUND BURKE, SELECTED WRITINGS AND SPEECHES ed Peter J. Stanlis (1997), cited by John O. McGinnis, *The Symbiosis of Constitutionalism and Technology*, 25 HARV. J. OF L. & PUBL. POLICY 3 (2001).

[137]See, for instance, the effect of file-sharing through the Internet has upon the laws of copyright; See Sonia K. Katyal, "Ending the revolution" (2002) 80(6) Texas Law Review 1465-1486.

necessarily hierarchical, or community-based.[139] The constitutional structure – and the legal system of which it forms a part – may be unsuited to coping with societal change wrought by this form of changing technology.[140]

All new technologies challenge existing legal concepts.[141] This operates at the micro level, as well as the macro. For instance, copyright law has been seriously affected by the advent of the Internet.[142] But technological changes can also help to produce relatively dramatic changes in economic

---

138

All mankind is of one author, and is one volume; when one man dies, one chapter is not torn out of the book, but translated into a better language; and every chapter must be so translated ... As therefore the bell that rings to a sermon, calls not upon the preacher only, but upon the congregation to come: so this bell calls us all: but how much more me, who am brought so near the door by this sickness .... No man is an island, entire of itself ... any man's death diminishes me, because I am involved in mankind; and therefore never send to know for whom the bell tolls; it tolls for thee."

– "Meditation XVII", from DEVOTIONS UPON EMERGENT OCCASIONS ed Anthony Raspa (1975).

This famous meditation of John Donne's puts forth two essential ideas which are representative of the Renaissance era in which it was written. The first (which is relevant here) is the idea that people are not isolated from one another, but that mankind is interconnected. The second is the vivid awareness of mortality that seems a natural outgrowth of a time when death was the constant companion of life.

[139]At least not necessarily upon the physical community.

[140]See Thomas G. Hermann, *Is U.S. legal system an impediment to scientific progress?*, 19 NATIONAL L. J. C-15 (4 August 1997). Not all would agree; see the law.com online seminar, *The Constitution and the Internet*, which considered the question "Can the Constitution Keep Up With the Internet?", at <http://www.law.com/jsp/statearchive.jsp?type=Article&oldid=ZZZRG Q220KC> (as at 6 December 2003).

[141]See Nasheri Hedieh, *The Intersection of technology crimes and cyberspace in Europe: The Case of Hungary*, 12 INFORM. & COMMS TECHN. L. 25 (2003).

[142]Neil Weinstock Netanel, *Copyright and a democratic civil society*, 106 YALE L. J. 283-387 (1996); David Friedman, *Does technology require new law?*, 25 HARV. J. OF L. & PUBL. POLICY 71-85 (2001) [Friedman discusses past technological changes relevant to copyright law and the law's response. He describes the technological changes that are now occurring or can be expected to occur over the next few decades, the issues they raise for the legal system and some possible responses].

and social organisation in a short span of time.[143] For moral as well as economic reasons, sound constitutions aim at promoting exchange and constraining hierarchy.[144] Constitutions are expected to provide stable rules suited to long-term use,[145] and social and economic accelleration makes this more difficult.

But constitutions are also affected by changes in technology, for the way in which a state is organised depends upon cultural and historical factors, which include the contemporary technology. Constitutions also depend upon technology because the structure of restraints on government most likely to produce justice[146] varies with the technology of the time.[147] A government powerful enough to protect liberty and property may be a government powerful enough to threaten liberty and property.[148] It is a question of balance.

The Lockean constitution was perceived as one which would be unalterable – because it encompassed all that was needed for a sound constitution.[149] This conception of a constitution has been challenged.[150] More importantly, perhaps, social and economic accelleration conflicts with the traditional expectation that constitutional law-makers can be expected to predict future trends with some measure of competence.[151]

Human history shows that at some point significant misalignment between the constitution and the social, economic, and political realities appears. This may cause fundamental departures from existing constitutional arrangements.[152] Constitutions risk becoming out of date,

---

[143]See MANUEL CASTELLS, THE RISE OF NETWORK SOCIETY (1996); William E. Scheuerman, *Constitutionalism in an age of speed*, 19 CONSTITUTIONAL COMMENTARY 353, 359-360 (2002).

[144]John O. McGinnis, *The Symbiosis of Constitutionalism and Technology*, 25 HARV. J. OF L. & PUBL. POLICY 3, 4 (2001).

[145]William E. Scheuerman, *Constitutionalism in an age of speed*, 19 CONSTITUTIONAL COMMENTARY 353, 360 (2002).

[146]Or whatever else may be seen as the ultimate aim of a constitution.

[147]See John O. McGinnis, *The Symbiosis of Constitutionalism and Technology*, 25 HARV. J. OF L. & PUBL. POLICY 3 (2001).

[148]See Barry Weingast, *The Economic Role of Political Institutions: Market Preserving Federalism and Economic Development*, 11 J. OF L. ECONOMICS & ORGANISATION 24-28 (1995).

[149]John Locke, *Fundamental Constitutions for Carolina*, in DAVID WOOTTON (ed), POLITICAL WRITINGS OF JOHN LOCKE, 232 (1993).

[150]William E. Scheuerman, *Constitutionalism in an age of speed*, 19 CONSTITUTIONAL COMMENTARY 353, 361 (2002).

[151]William E. Scheuerman, *Constitutionalism in an age of speed*, 19 CONSTITUTIONAL COMMENTARY 353, 362 (2002).

when "all fixed, fast-frozen relations, with their train of ancient and venerable prejudices and opinions, are swept away, all new-formed ones become antiquated before they can ossify."[153] Contemporary conditions require constitutions exhibiting enormous flexibility; they now must leave room for a vast and constantly expanding range of novel social and economic experiences, many of which may prove momentous.[154]

Changes in the past

This section will briefly examine several seminal technological changes which have occurred in the past, in an attempt to identify the effect these had upon constitutions, and, to a lesser extent, the ways in which they may have been influenced in their development by the nature and form of the constitution.

The first technological change which will be considered is the early development of civilisation. Inundation – as of the Nile Valley through the annual flooding – led to cultivation, as it encouraged intensive agriculture.[155] But the precarious nature of the flood – too much and the soil would be washed away, too little and there would be insufficient to ensure a harvest – required strong government, including the use of levies for public works, writing and record-keeping, and of taxation.[156] The waters had to be harnessed. In Egypt, the Pharaoh also owed his[157] pre-eminence to his

---

[152]Richard Kay, *Constitutional Chrononomy*, 13 RATIO JURIS 31, 41 (2000).

[153]Friedrich Engels to Karl Marx, *Manifesto of the Communist Party*, in ROBERT C. TUCKER, THE MARX-ENGELS READER, 469 (1972).

[154]William E. Scheuerman, *Constitutionalism in an age of speed*, 19 CONSTITUTIONAL COMMENTARY 353, 365 (2002).

[155]See Robert C. Allen, *Agriculture and the origins of the state in ancient Egypt*, 34 EXPLORATIONS IN ECONOMIC HISTORY 135-154 (1997); Arthur Mirsky, *Influence of geologic factors on ancient Egyptian civilisation*, 45 J. OF GEOSCIENCE EDUCATION 415 (1997) [Allen, in particular, argues that, in Egypt, state formation occurred much more rapidly after the adoption of farming than in many other parts of the ancient Near East, and the Egyptian state lasted longer and was more stable than most empires established elsewhere. He argues that successful states in the ancient world depended on the ability of elites to extract a surplus from farmers and other producers].

[156]See, generally, DAVID A. WARBURTON, STATE AND ECONOMY IN ANCIENT EGYPT: FISCAL VOCABULARY OF THE NEW KINGDOM (1997).

[157]Hatchepsut, in the eighteenth dynasty, ruled as a female Pharaoh, not as a queen regnant. Cleopatra, and others of her Macedonian Lagidæ line, were of the post-dynastic Ptolemaic era; see JOYCE TYLDESLEY, HATCHEPSUT:

control of the army,[158] which in itself may be seen as mastery of technology having constitutional consequences. Loss of crops due to a failure in the flood (or excessive flooding)[159] could, and sometimes did, lead to political change.[160] For example, between the Middle and the New Kingdoms, beginning about 1700 BC (the Second Intermediate Period), a series of unpredictable floods struck the Nile and Egypt, and at least partly as a result of this failure of technology,[161] fragmented into two kingdoms.[162]

Egypt's geopolitics were both similar to and different from Mesopotamia's.[163] Both cultures evolved in hot dry river valleys that required irrigation, which in turn required organisation and a strong government that led to civilisation.[164] In fact, Egyptians depended so much on irrigation and the high level of organisation and authority needed to

---

THE FEMALE PHARAOH (1996); MICHEL CHAUVEAU; CLEOPATRA: BEYOND THE MYTH trans David Lorton (2002).

[158]See NIGEL STRUDWICK, THE ADMINISTRATION OF EGYPT IN THE OLD KINGDOM: THE HIGHEST TITLES AND THEIR HOLDERS (1985).

[159]The Egyptians realised quite well that their prosperity and welfare depended on the Nile which provided its people with most of what they needed to survive: fish and wildlife, mud for building materials, a "highway" for easy transportation, and papyrus for paper. Most importantly, the Nile floods annually from June to October, watering the ground and replenishing the soil with a rich fertile layer of silt. The Egyptians called their land kmt ("the Black land") after this layer of silt. The real essence of Egypt consisted of a long thin strip of land along the Nile that was never more than a few kilometres wide. Outside of this strip was the "Red land", the desert.

[160]The ten plagues of Egypt could be seen as an example of technology having constitutional effects – Moses and the elders of Israel contended with the priests of Egypt for mastery (Exodus, 7-10); See Richard D. Patterson, *Wonders in the heavens and on the earth: Apocalyptic imagery in the Old Testament*, 43 J. OF THE EVANGELICAL THEOLOGICAL SOCIETY 385 (2000).

[161]This was not merely a failure of nature, for the annual innundation was merely the first part of a technological process largely controlled by the state.

[162]See Anthony Spalinger, *The Political Situation in Egypt during the Second Intermediate Period, c.1800-1550 BC*, 60 J. OF NEAR EASTERN STUDIES 296 (2001).

[163]See GWENDOLYN LEICK, MESOPOTAMIA: THE INVENTION OF THE CITY (2001).

[164]See DAVID WARBURTON, EGYPT AND THE NEAR EAST: POLITICS IN THE BRONZE AGE (2001); BRUCE G. TRIGGER, EARLY CIVILISATIONS: ANCIENT EGYPT IN CONTEXT (1993).

maintain it that they considered their rulers, the Pharaohs, gods.[165] The power and effectiveness of these god-kings corresponded directly to Egypt's prosperity, which itself depended on the floods' regularity and the effectiveness of the irrigation system which was required to take advantage of it.[166] The control of agricultural technology led to a strongly centralised government – and in turn the centralised government fostered intensive agriculture which depended upon careful use of the available technology.[167]

The Roman Empire was also dependent upon technology for its political survival, which therefore influenced the nature and form of the constitution.[168] The key here, for an empire which lacked a clearly defined border such as Egypt had,[169] was communications. As McGinnis has noted, one of the most important ways in which technology transforms the environment is by reducing transportation and communication costs.[170] Such reductions made possible new forms of constitutional structures[171] –

---

[165]See REGINE SCHULZ & MATTHIAS SEIDEL (eds), EGYPT: THE WORLD OF THE PHARAOHS (1998). Whilst the Mesopotamian rulers were also seen as gods, this might be seen as due to the need for the people to have an intermediary with the gods not dwelling on earth. More importantly, each city boasted its own god-king, and there was no comparable unity as found in Egypt; H.I.H. Prince Takahito Mikasa (ed), *Monarchies and socio-religious traditions in the ancient Near East*: PAPERS READ AT THE 31ST INTERNATIONAL CONGRESS OF HUMAN SCIENCES IN ASIA AND NORTH AFRICA (1984).

[166]See Robert C. Allen, *Agriculture and the origins of the state in ancient Egypt*, 34 EXPLORATIONS IN ECONOMIC HISTORY 135-154 (1997).

[167]Here, technology is largely agricultural, in particular the use of irrigation. Other major civilisations have also depended upon irrigation – or been created by them – as, for example, the Khmer kingdom; See CHARLES HIGHAM, THE CIVILISATION OF ANGKOR (2001).

[168]The law in general was also influenced by economic and social factors; See JEAN-JACQUES AUBERT & BOUDEWIJN SIRKS (eds), SPECULUM IURIS: ROMAN LAW AS A REFLECTION OF SOCIAL AND ECONOMIC LIFE IN ANTIQUITY (2002).

[169]Most other civilisations such as the Tigris-Euphrates, and Indus valleys in the Old World and the Valley of Mexico and the mountain and coastal valleys of Peru in the New World also enjoyed defined borders – even if, like Mesopotamia, and the Indus valley, it was a water catchment area. See also Robert L. Carneiro, *A Theory of the Origin of the State*, 169 SCIENCE 733, 734 (1970).

[170]John O. McGinnis, *The Symbiosis of Constitutionalism and Technology*, 25 HARV. J. OF L. & PUBL. POLICY 3, 6 (2001).

[171]John O. McGinnis, *The Symbiosis of Constitutionalism and Technology*, 25

in the case of Rome – an empire.[172] Indeed, it depended upon these communications systems for its survival, as the size of the empire meant that military forces had to be moved swiftly wherever necessary to meet a new threat.[173]

In the Roman world this included roads,[174] military networks,[175] and system of civil and military administration – including the legal system.[176] This involved a degree of constitutional centralisation,[177] but occasionally this failed.[178] This was less serious that might perhaps otherwise have been the case, because the next constitutional tier below the imperial government were the provinces, which were run as part of a relatively homogenous imperial system.[179] In the later period of the empire, fiscal, military, and

---

HARV. J. OF L. & PUBL. POLICY 3, 6 (2001).

[172]While not the first empire in Europe – that distinction might go to Alexandra, or to the Minoans (or any of a number of earlier peoples), it was the first viable multinational empire. See CLIFFORD ANDO, IMPERIAL IDEOLOGY AND PROVINCIAL LOYALTY IN THE ROMAN EMPIRE (2000); S.E. FINER, THE HISTORY OF GOVERNMENT FROM THE EARLIEST TIMES (1997).

[173]See THOMAS S. BURNS, BARBARIANS WITHIN THE GATES OF ROME: A STUDY OF ROMAN MILITARY POLICY AND THE BARBARIANS, CA. 375-425 A.D (1994).

[174]See RAYMOND CHEVALLIER, ROMAN ROADS trans by N.H. Field (1976).

[175]See, for instance, D.J. WOOLLISCROFT, ROMAN MILITARY SIGNALLING (2001).

[176]See JEAN-JACQUES AUBERT AND BOUDEWIJN SIRKS (eds), SPECULUM IURIS: ROMAN LAW AS A REFLECTION OF SOCIAL AND ECONOMIC LIFE IN ANTIQUITY (2002). Roman law forms the basis of the civil law system, which is one of the principle legal systems in use today.

[177]This was especially so after the evolution of the imperial constitution – such as it was – through the adoption of the eastern model of divine ruler. See J. RUFUS FEARS, PRINCEPS A DIIS ELECTUS: THE DIVINE ELECTION OF THE EMPEROR AS A POLITICAL CONCEPT AT ROME (1977).

[178]There was, for instance, no satisfactory imperial succession law; See J. RUFUS FEARS, PRINCEPS A DIIS ELECTUS: THE DIVINE ELECTION OF THE EMPEROR AS A POLITICAL CONCEPT AT ROME (1977). When the succession was disputed provincial governors, or generals, might contend for the imperial purple. See, for example, in the year of the three emperors; JOHN GRAINGER, NERVA AND THE ROMAN SUCCESSION CRISIS OF AD 96-99 (2003).

[179]See ANDREW LINTOTT, IMPERIUM ROMANUM: POLITICS AND ADMINISTRATION (1993). Governors might vie for the purple, but rarely

population collapse[180] led to the empire being divided, first temporarily and eventually permanently, into east and west.[181] Yet, while the communications systems were operating, Rome was able to oversee – if not always aid – provinces many hundreds of kilometres away.[182] Unfortunately, because the mechanisms through which the empire operated depended greatly upon the army, and particularly because the formal constitutional powers of the emperors' were long disguised, the army was often to assume a political role.[183] With politico-strategic changes – including an increased emphasis upon the eastern borders, meant that a single government was incapable of effectively administering the whole empire.

Communications and transportation technology had allowed the Roman empire to be run in a centralised fashion.[184] As utilisation of technology declined in effectiveness – partly through over-commitment – decentralisation increased.[185] Technology, of this type, made a significant contribution to the form of the imperial Roman constitution and was

---

would a province secede for very long.

[180]See F.W. WALBANK, THE AWFUL REVOLUTION: THE DECLINE OF THE ROMAN EMPIRE IN THE WEST (1969).

[181]See TIMOTHY D. BARNES, THE NEW EMPIRE OF DIOCLETIAN AND CONSTANTINE (1982).

[182]This was at least until the conditions facing the imperial heartlands rendered all contact – and aid – uncertain. See, for instance, VENERABLE BEDE, BEDE'S ECCLESIASTICAL HISTORY OF THE ENGLISH PEOPLE: A HISTORICAL COMMENTARY ed J.M. Wallace-Hadrill chapter XIII (1988):

To Agitius (Aetius), thrice consul, the Groans of the Britons ... the barbarians drive us to the sea, the sea drives us to the barbarians; between these two means of death we are either killed or drowned. There is no reply.

– from *The Groans of the Britains* (446AD). By Agitius Gildas presumably meant Aetius. Aetius held his third consulship from 446 to 454.

[183]See J.B. CAMPBELL, THE EMPEROR AND THE ROMAN ARMY, 31 BC-AD 235 (1984); LUCAS DE BLOIS, THE ROMAN ARMY AND POLITICS IN THE FIRST CENTURY BEFORE CHRIST (1987).

[184]Aqueducts, public granaries, etc allowed the city of Rome to become a metropolis of at least half a million people; See Harry B. Evans, *The Water Supply of Ancient Rome: City Area, Water, and Population*, 94 ISIS 360 (2003); Glenn R. Storey, *The population of ancient Rome*, 71 ANTIQUITY 966 (1997).

[185]Aquaducts failed, secure food supplies dwindled, people left the cities, causing a decline of the city-state government; See Robert Coates-Stephens, *The walls and aqueducts of Rome in the early Middle Ages, A.D. 500-1000*, 88 THE J. OF ROMAN STUDIES 166 (1998).

fostered by a regime built on public works and military technology.

The Dark Ages after the collapse of the Roman empire in the west, and the Middle Ages which followed, were a time when the weakness of communications contributed to the division of states, and eventually to feudalism.[186] Feudalism was a political, social, and economic system founded upon the conditions of the time – including technological limitations (especially transportation and communications).[187] These constitutional arrangements relied upon a hierarchical structure of political, social and economic obligations.[188] It might be said to be a type of Lockean constitution, with individuals and communities linked for mutual protection.[189] The limitations of technology meant that the constitutional arrangements were restricted in scope, and decentralisation was common in this era – even for a state such as England, which generally lacked the over-mighty baronage more common on the continent of Europe,[190] and which enjoyed an unusually sophisticated fiscal system from late Saxon times.[191]

---

[186]See F.M. STENTON, THE FIRST CENTURY OF ENGLISH FEUDALISM (1961); J.M.W. BEAN, THE DECLINE OF ENGLISH FEUDALISM, 1215-1540 (1968); JEROME BLUM, THE END OF THE OLD ORDER IN RURAL EUROPE (1978).

[187]See, for instance, FERDINAND LOT, THE END OF THE ANCIENT WORLD AND THE BEGINNINGS OF THE MIDDLE AGES (1953); F.M. STENTON, THE FIRST CENTURY OF ENGLISH FEUDALISM (1961); J.M.W. BEAN, THE DECLINE OF ENGLISH FEUDALISM, 1215-1540 (1968); JEROME BLUM, THE END OF THE OLD ORDER IN RURAL EUROPE (1978).

[188]See BRIAN TIERNEY, RELIGION, LAW, AND THE GROWTH OF CONSTITUTIONAL THOUGHT, 1150-1650 (1982); KENNETH PENNINGTON, THE PRINCE AND THE LAW, 1200-1600: SOVEREIGNTY AND RIGHTS IN THE WESTERN LEGAL TRADITION (1993); THOMAS ERTMAN, BIRTH OF THE LEVIATHAN: BUILDING STATES AND REGIMES IN MEDIÆVAL AND EARLY MODERN EUROPE (1997); HEINRICH MITTELS, THE STATE IN THE MIDDLE AGES: A COMPARATIVE CONSTITUTIONAL HISTORY OF FEUDAL EUROPE trans H.F. ORTON (1975).

[189]See JOHN HUDSON, LAND, LAW, AND LORDSHIP IN ANGLO-NORMAN ENGLAND (1994). There were however signs of a more complex form of constitution emerging; See ARTHUR P. MONAHAN, CONSENT, COERCION, AND LIMIT: THE MEDIÆVAL ORIGINS OF PARLIAMENTARY DEMOCRACY (1987).

[190]See JONATHAN DEWALD, THE EUROPEAN NOBILITY, 1400-1800 (1996). See also RICHARD GORSKI, THE FOURTEENTH-CENTURY SHERIFF: ENGLISH LOCAL ADMINISTRATION IN THE LATE MIDDLE AGES (2003).

[191]See HENRY LOYN, THE GOVERNANCE OF ANGLO-SAXON ENGLAND, 500-1087 (1984).

There were of course technological influences upon the constitution, and upon society in general, including the gradually increasing rate of literacy, and the consequent spread of new political – and religious – ideas.[192] These were eventually to lead to a profound religious and political revolution – and to technological and constitutional change.

The Reformation, in contrast to the Middle Ages, was a time of significant technological change. In part this was caused by such inventions as the printing press,[193] but it was also a result of increased trade with the east,[194] and the importation of new ideas (including from the classical world, and Islam), from as early as the first crusade.[195] These changes led to changing perceptions of the role of the state (including the rise of a belief in a social compact between state and individual, or state and community).[196] It is less clear than for ancient and classical Egypt that these changes were as a result of technological changes, or whether the technological changes led to social changes, which in turn led to constitutional changes.[197] Yet the

---

[192]See JEAN GIMPEL, THE MEDIÆVAL MACHINE: THE INDUSTRIAL REVOLUTION OF THE MIDDLE AGES (1977); STEVEN JUSTICE, WRITING AND REBELLION: ENGLAND IN 1381 (1994).

[193]See JOHN MAN, THE GUTENBERG REVOLUTION: THE STORY OF A GENIUS AND AN INVENTION THAT CHANGED THE WORLD (2002). For a slightly later period see DAVID ZARET, ORIGINS OF DEMOCRATIC CULTURE: PRINTING, PETITIONS, AND THE PUBLIC SPHERE IN EARLY-MODERN ENGLAND (2000); ALEXANDRA HALASZ, THE MARKETPLACE OF PRINT: PAMPHLETS AND THE PUBLIC SPHERE IN EARLY MODERN ENGLAND (1997).

[194]Including with Byzantium, the heart of the eastern empire; See DENO JOHN GEANAKOPLOS, CONSTANTINOPLE AND THE WEST: ESSAYS ON THE LATE BYZANTINE (PALAEOLOGAN) AND ITALIAN RENAISSANCES AND THE BYZANTINE AND ROMAN CHURCHES (1989); KRIJNIE N. CIGGAAR, WESTERN TRAVELLERS TO CONSTANTINOPLE: THE WEST AND BYZANTIUM, 962-1204: CULTURAL AND POLITICAL RELATIONS (1996).

[195]See AZIZ SURYAL ATIYA, CRUSADE, COMMERCE AND CULTURE (1962); VLADIMIR P. GOSS & CHRISTINE VERZAIR BORNSTEIN (eds), THE MEETING OF TWO WORLDS: CULTURAL EXCHANGE BETWEEN EAST AND WEST DURING THE PERIOD OF THE CRUSADES (1986).

[196]See DAVID BOUCHER & PAUL KELLY (eds), THE SOCIAL CONTRACT FROM HOBBES TO RAWLS (1994); PATRICK RILEY, WILL AND POLITICAL LEGITIMACY: A CRITICAL EXPOSITION OF SOCIAL CONTRACT THEORY IN HOBBES, LOCKE, ROUSSEAU, KANT, AND HEGEL (1982); MARTYN P. THOMPSON, IDEAS OF CONTRACT IN ENGLISH POLITICAL THOUGHT IN THE AGE OF JOHN LOCKE (1987).

[197]It is probably both working together. The spread of knowledge led to

example of the Reformation shows us that even in relatively complex societies constitutions may be effected by technology. Technology itself continued to develop, particularly where constitutions, and societies, were more liberal.[198]

The invention of the printing press encouraged the circulation of information, which in turn encouraged the development of common politics beyond the immediate community.[199] This spreading of knowledge was to have a major role in German, and somewhat later, Italian re-unification.[200] The modern territorial state was unknown to antiquity and to the middle ages, except in those cities which alone saw sufficient division of labour and concentration in a confined area.[201] But with the advent of the printing press it was possible to transmit, preserve, and utilise large quantities of information. This was soon used by government bureaucracies, which sought to record as much information as they could – initially often for taxation purposes – but later for other purposes also, as the scope of government – and the complexity of the constitution – grew.[202]

The Reformation did not, of course, effect countries equally, and it was confined to Europe. It passed through various stages – including the Counter-Reformation – which itself saw a blossoming of constitutional theory,[203] though this was mostly driven by political and religious forces.

Somewhat later the Industrial Revolution, which saw the true advent of mass manufacture, led to greater population size and higher productivity

---

greater awareness, and greater demands. But it is also true that these tools were also utilised by the state, and this subtly changed the ways in which it operated. For instance, the increased administrative efficiency of central government encouraged centralisation. See, for example, the decline of the offices of sheriff and coroner; See JUDITH A. GREEN, ENGLISH SHERIFFS TO 1154 (1990); RICHARD GORSKI, THE FOURTEENTH-CENTURY SHERIFF: ENGLISH LOCAL ADMINISTRATION IN THE LATE MIDDLE AGES (2003); R.F. HUNNISETT, THE MEDIÆVAL CORONER (1961).

[198]As generally in England, and the Protestant parts of Europe.

[199]See JOSEPH LOEWENSTEIN, THE AUTHOR'S DUE: PRINTING AND THE PREHISTORY OF COPYRIGHT (2002).

[200]John O. McGinnis, *The Symbiosis of Constitutionalism and Technology*, 25 HARV. J. OF L. & PUBL. POLICY 3, 6 (2001); See also Detlev F. Vagts, *State Succession: The Codifiers View*, 33 VIRGINIA J. OF INTERN. L. 275 (1993).

[201]Hermann Heller, *The Decline of the Nation State and its Effect on Constitutional and International Economic Law*, 18 CARDOZO L. REV. 1139, 1142 (1996).

[202]See M.T. CLANCHY, FROM MEMORY TO WRITTEN RECORD, ENGLAND 1066-1307 (1993).

[203]See MICHAEL A. MULLETT, THE CATHOLIC REFORMATION (1999); NICHOLAS S. DAVIDSON, THE COUNTER-REFORMATION (1987).

and rapid economic growth.[204] Most social theorists agree that the ascent of industrial capitalism in the nineteenth century unleashed a particularly intense period of social and economic accelleration.[205] This led to more taxation revenue for the government, but also to more social and economic problems,[206] and so larger scope for government intervention.[207] This in turn led in turn to greater demands for democracy, such as was manifested by the chartists and the electoral reformers in the U.K. during the early nineteenth century.[208] But domestic economic policies remained largely laissez-faire, which encouraged further development.[209]

It may well be that it was economic and social changes, wrought by technological advances, which resulted in constitutional changes during the Industrial Revolution – domestically at least this was possibly true.[210] But the development of colonial empires in the course of the nineteenth century seems to have been due, in part at least, to the direct effect of technology, more narrowly defined. Naval and military technology enabled colonial powers to build empires in places once beyond their reach.[211] The very

---

[204]See SIDNEY POLLARD, ESSAYS ON THE INDUSTRIAL REVOLUTION IN BRITAIN ed Colin Holmes (2000); MARGARET C. JACOB, SCIENTIFIC CULTURE AND THE MAKING OF THE INDUSTRIAL WEST (1997).

[205]William E. Scheuerman, *Constitutionalism in an age of speed*, 19 CONSTITUTIONAL COMMENTARY 353, 357-358 (2002). Koselleck highlights key aspects of early modern history, including innovations in transportation and communications inspired by mercantilism, as motivating forces behind much of this development; REINHART KOSELLECK, ZEITSCHICHTEN, 157-158 (2000).

[206]See, PAUL SLACK, THE ENGLISH POOR LAW, 1531-1782 (1995).

[207]See ARTHUR J. TAYLOR, LAISSEZ-FAIRE AND STATE INTERVENTION IN NINETEENTH-CENTURY BRITAIN (1972); SIR NORMAN CHESTER, THE ENGLISH ADMINISTRATIVE SYSTEM, 1780-1870 (1981). See also ROY MACLEOD (ed), GOVERNMENT AND EXPERTISE: SPECIALISTS, ADMINISTRATORS, AND PROFESSIONALS, 1860-1919 (1988); BERNARD S. SILBERMAN, CAGES OF REASON: THE RISE OF THE RATIONAL STATE IN FRANCE, JAPAN, THE UNITED STATES, AND GREAT BRITAIN (1993).

[208]See NANCY D. LOPATIN, POLITICAL UNIONS, POPULAR POLITICS AND THE GREAT REFORM ACT OF 1832 (1999); JOHN CHARLTON, THE CHARTISTS: THE FIRST NATIONAL WORKERS' MOVEMENT (1997).

[209]See ARTHUR J. TAYLOR, LAISSEZ-FAIRE AND STATE INTERVENTION IN NINETEENTH-CENTURY BRITAIN (1972).

[210]Though it could equally be said that it was the social changes which led to constitutional changes – particularly the growth in disparity between those places represented in Parliament, and those which had the largest populations; See JOHN K. WALTON, THE SECOND REFORM ACT (1987).

needs of those naval forces led to further expansion, as for example, the building of coaling stations across the globe.[212] Like the Roman empire, these new empires relied heavily upon communications. The telegraph,[213] seabed cables, and fast shipping[214] meant that an empire could encompass the globe, and yet be administered – without too much difficulty – from the imperial heartland.[215] There was a considerable degree of de-centralisation, which was to increase as colonial territories developed more fully.[216] But the oversight of territories changed the nature of domestic political structures – for example, in the British experience, the Crown – considerably.[217]

The Industrial Revolution gave economic power to those counties in which it began – particularly the U.K. – but it also gave them technological advantages which meant that they enjoyed political advantages.[218] These

---

[211]See WOODRUFF D. SMITH, EUROPEAN IMPERIALISM IN THE NINETEENTH AND TWENTIETH CENTURIES (1982).

[212]For an illustration of these, see ADAM KIRKALDY, BRITISH SHIPPING: ITS HISTORY, ORGANISATION AND IMPORTANCE, WITH A MAP OF MAIN ROUTES AND COALING STATIONS AND FULL APPENDICES (1914).

[213]See TOM STANDAGE, THE VICTORIAN INTERNET: THE REMARKABLE STORY OF THE TELEGRAPH AND THE NINETEENTH CENTURY'S ONLINE PIONEERS (1999).

[214]Note also that the development of an effective chronometer, and the invention of longitude, did much to open up the world's oceans in the eighteenth century; DAVA SOBEL, LONGITUDE: THE TRUE STORY OF A LONE GENIUS WHO SOLVED THE GREATEST SCIENTIFIC PROBLEM OF HIS TIME (1995).

[215]See ALPHEUS H SNOW, THE ADMINISTRATION OF DEPENDENCIES: A STUDY OF THE EVOLUTION OF THE FEDERAL EMPIRE, WITH SPECIAL REFERENCE TO AMERICAN COLONIAL PROBLEMS (1902); ANALYSIS OF THE SYSTEM OF GOVERNMENT THROUGHOUT THE BRITISH EMPIRE (1912); JOHN W. CELL, BRITISH COLONIAL ADMINISTRATION IN THE MID-NINETEENTH CENTURY: THE POLICY-MAKING PROCESS (1970); CEDRIC LOWE, THE RELUCTANT IMPERIALISTS: BRITISH FOREIGN POLICY, 1878-1902 (1967).

[216]See, for instance, Noel Cox, *The control of advice to the Crown and the development of executive independence in New Zealand*, 13 BOND L. REV. 166-189 (2001).

[217]See George Winterton, *The evolution of a separate Australian crown*, 19 MONASH UNIV. L. REV. 1-22 (1993); Noel Cox, *The control of advice to the Crown and the development of executive independence in New Zealand*, 13(1) BOND L. REV. 166-189 (2001). The office of secretary of state also evolved over time, partly as a consequence of greater emphasis upon external affairs; DAVID KYNASTON, THE SECRETARY OF STATE (1978).

resulted in constitutional changes, including a focus on empire, a rapid development in social and educational policies and the scope and reach of government generally, and greater democracy.[219]

Each of the above technological and historical periods were marked by quite different technological, economic, social, political and constitutional features. In some cases, such as Egypt, the Reformation, and during the Industrial Revolution, it is comparatively easy to see how technological change effected society, and therefore the constitution. Even in the Roman empire, and during the Middle Ages, there were signs that this was also occurring. That technology changes society, and society changes the constitution, may be a commonplace. But we can see signs that technology has directly affected the constitution, while perhaps also having social or economic effects. These may perhaps be seen in the way in which Egypt required strong government or she would not have survived, that Rome would not have established a lasting empire except through effective communications, and the development of colonial empires by the European powers in the nineteenth century.[220]

Some technological changes have directed effected the constitution, others have not – but it seems that when this has occurred it has been in respect of foreign policy, rather more often than domestic, except in the more primative societies. It would also seem that technology itself develops when government requires it (as in Egypt), or where the constitution is sufficiently laissez-faire to allow people the freedom to development technology. It may be that seminal changes which have a direct impact of the structure of the constitution will be rare – particularly as the complexity of society increases. Whether these examples give us any guidance to the future we will leave until after considering some contemporary technological revolutions.

---

[218]As exemplified in the era of "gunboat diplomacy", for instance, MIRIAM HOOD, GUNBOAT DIPLOMACY, 1895-1905: GREAT POWER PRESSURE IN VENEZUELA (1975).

[219]See, for instance, the 1848 revolutions on the European continent; RUDOLF STADELMANN, SOCIAL AND POLITICAL HISTORY OF THE GERMAN 1848 REVOLUTION trans J.G. Chastain (1975).

[220]These may be compared with the development of the US in the nineteenth century, which was accellerated by the construction of the railways, and – somewhat earlier – states and empires such as Zimbabwe, built upon gold-mining; See INNOCENT PIKIRAYI, THE ZIMBABWE CULTURE: ORIGINS AND DECLINE OF SOUTHERN ZAMBEZIAN STATES (2001).

Changes in the present

We will now look at several contemporary technological revolutions, in an attempt to identify the effect these are having upon constitutions. Because the current technological revolution is essentially a "knowledge revolution," the two examples which will be used are both of this type – telecommunications, and the Internet.[221]

(a) Telecommunications

The movement toward deregulation of telecommunications is a worldwide phenomenon, though there is little or no general pattern.[222] But the revolution in information technology is arguably changing society fundamentally, and will probably continue to do so in the foreseeable future.[223] This is having significant economic and social effects, but it is not yet clear that there are constitutional effects.

The infrastructure of an information society[224] will have social, economic and political aspects – and it is only with the latter that we are here concerned. Computers and information technology such as telecommunications and management science models for decision-making are commonly used by government agencies.[225] They effect the relationships between the organs of government, but could, in Kraemer's view, danger personal privacy and political elections, and, to a lesser extent, the separation of powers and (American) federalism.[226] The reasons for this lie in the fact that telecommunications lead to faster communications and

---

[221]Biotechnology and genetics are similar, but there the effects may be more social and ethical than constitutional.

[222]See David Lazer and Viktor Mayer-Schonberger, *Governing networks: telecommunication deregulation in Europe and the United States*, 27 BROOKLYN J. OF INTERN'L L. 819-851 (2002).

[223]See Nasheri Hedieh, *The Intersection of technology crimes and cyberspace in Europe: The Case of Hungary*, 12 INFORM. & COMMS. TECHN. L. 25 (2003).

[224]See BAHAA EL-HADIDY & ESTHER E. HORNE (eds), THE INFRASTRUCTURE OF AN INFORMATION SOCIETY: PROCEEDINGS OF THE FIRST INTERNATIONAL INFORMATION CONFERENCE IN EGYPT, CAIRO, 13-15 DECEMBER, 1982 (1982).

[225]See Kenneth L. Kraemer, *Computers and the Constitution: A Helpful, Harmful or Harmless Relationship?*, 47 PUBL. ADMIN. REV. 93-105 (1987).

[226]See Kenneth L. Kraemer, *Computers and the Constitution: A Helpful, Harmful or Harmless Relationship?*, 47(1) PUBL. ADMIN. REV. 93-105 (1987).

less need for intermediate levels of government – and therefore an increasingly focus on the centre. We will look at but one example of this.

McGinnis argues that the U.S. constitution, while at the heart of the steady growth of the US, helping it to become an economic superpower by the beginning of the twentieth century, contained within itself the seeds of its own destruction.[227] The drop in transportation costs undermined the core attachment of citizens to their states, what was seen as a necessary condition for federalism to resist dissolution by interest groups.[228] This has been exacerbated by the advent of modern telecommunications. In the US, this has led to a decline in the enumerated powers – those reserved to the states at the expense of the federal government – through judgments of the U.S. Supreme Court, principally as a reaction to technological changes.[229] Thus the balance between federal and state powers, which has been characterised as a key to economic success, was changed, in McGinnis' view, because of the advent of telecommunications.[230]

But is this technology changing society, which therefore results in changes to the law, or is it technology directly changing the constitution? Because of the mode of change in McGinnis' model – U.S. Supreme Court constitutional exegesis[231] – it could arguably be more the latter than the former. However, it would be unwise to attempt to identify too clearly a distinction between technology changing society, and society changing the constitution, and technology changing the constitution, for in practice both technology and society are at work simultaneously upon the constitution.[232] It may be, however, that the centralising tendency of telecommunications, of which McGinnis wrote, is affecting the constitution as directly as is possible in a complex modern society.

---

[227]John O. McGinnis, *The Symbiosis of Constitutionalism and Technology*, 25 HARV. J. OF L. & PUBL. POLICY 3, 6-7 (2001).

[228]John O. McGinnis, *The Symbiosis of Constitutionalism and Technology*, 25 HARV. J. OF L. & PUBL. POLICY 3, 7 (2001). See also John O. McGinnis, *The Original Constitution and Our Origins*, 19 HARV. J. OF L. & PUBL. POLICY 251, 253 (1995).

[229]John O. McGinnis, *The Symbiosis of Constitutionalism and Technology*, 25 HARV. J. OF L. & PUBL. POLICY 3, 8 (2001). Note that this reform is through judicial interpretation rather than constitutional amendment.

[230]See John O. McGinnis, *The Symbiosis of Constitutionalism and Technology*, 25 HARV. J. OF L. & PUBL. POLICY 3 (2001).

[231]For which see Nickolai G. Levin, *Constitutional statutory synthesis*, 54 ALABAMA L. REV. 1281-1373 (2003).

[232]Though the balance may vary over time, and from place to place.

(b) The Internet

The regulation of the Internet is an especially important example in our study.[233] It has been said that the very nature and growing importance of the Internet requires a fundamental re-examination of the constitutional structure within which rule-making takes place.[234] The Internet, or cyberspace, may be seen to have an opposite effect to the centralising effect of telecommunications (as everyone has access to data everyone can join new communities, leading to an decentralising effect). Yet Internet-based direct democracy is theoretically possible,[235] as is globalisation – the ultimate in centralisation. These are clearly more than merely economic or social effects – they strike at the core of the constitution – but it remains to be seen precisely what the constitutional effects of the Internet will be. These will probably vary depending upon the level of Internet exposure, and the relative complexity and rigidity of each country's constitution.[236]

We will begin with a definition of the Internet. The Internet, or "cyberspace", is an interconnected electronic communications network. It has no physical existence as a whole, though comprised of a large number of individual networks.[237] In essence the Internet exists in a virtual world, rather than in the real, geographical, world.[238] The Internet has no

---

[233]It may be accepted that regulation of some form is necessary, if only to protect consumers; See Jessica Bagner, Vanessa Kaye Watson & K Brooke Welch, *Internet auction fraud targeted by FTC, state and local law enforcement officials*, 15 INTELLECTUAL PROPERTY & TECHN. L. J. 22 (2003) [The U.S. Federal Trade Commission ("FTC") logged more than 51,000 auction complaints in 2002, and auction fraud is the single largest category of Internet-related complaints].

[234]See David R. Johnson & David G. Post, *And How Shall the Net be Governed? A Meditation on the Relative Virtues of Decentralised, Emergent Law*, draft paper at Cyberspace Law Institute Papers on Cyberspace Law, available at <http://www.cli.org/emdraft.html> (as at 28 November 2003).

[235]See Bruce E. Cain, *The Internet in the (dis)service of democracy?*, 34 LOYOLA OF LOS ANGELES L. REV. 1005-1021 (2001).

[236]There is a tendency to look only at examples from one's own country.

[237]The result being a conceptual confusion: see Jack L. Goldsmith & Lawrence Lessig, *Grounding the Virtual Magistrate*, available at <http://www.lessig.org/content/articles/works/magistrate.html> (as at 28 November 2003).

[238]See Georgios Zekos, *Internet or Electronic Technology: A Threat to State Sovereignty*, 3 J. OF INFORM., L. & TECHN. (1999), available at <http://elj.warwick.ac.UK/jilt/99-3/zekos.html> (as at 28 November 2003); David G. Post & David R. Johnson, *'Chaos Prevailing on Every*

controlling body,[239] although it does have a common language, allowing different operating systems to speak to one another.[240] In essence, it is a facilitator, a means by which computers may be linked, but its effect goes very much further.

It might be asked why the Internet presents particular difficulties for society, economy and constitution. Largely, it would appear that this is because of its global reach into homes, and its universality and immediacy. It is possible, for the first time, for traders to reach consumers directly, without any intermediaries.[241] It might even be possible to bypass national laws altogether. A state created on the Internet – were such a thing possible – would have no corporeal existence, yet it may be no less real for that.

Continent': Towards a New Theory of Decentralised Decision-Making in Complex Systems, 14 June 1999, Social Science Research Network Electronic Library, available   at <http://papers.ssrn.com/sol3/delivery.cfm/99032613.pdf?abstractid=157 692> (as at 1 December 2003). See also Dan L. Burk, *Federalism in Cyberspace,* 28 Connecticut L. Rev. 1095 (1996); Joel R. Reidenberg, *Governing Networks and Rule-Making in_Cyberspace,* in BRIAN KAHIN & CHARLES NESSON (eds), BORDERS IN CYBERSPACE 84, 85-87 (1996).

[239]Though the Internet Corporation for Assigned Names and Numbers (ICANN) regulates some aspects of the net. This is the non-profit corporation that was formed to assume responsibility for the Internet Protocol (IP) address space allocation, protocol parameter assignment, domain name system management, and root server system management functions previously performed under U.S. Government contract by Internet Assigned Numbers Authority (IANA) and other entities. That no single country can regulate the Internet is seen in the internationalisation of ICANN. See for instance, James S. Fishkin, *Deliberate Polling As a Model for ICANN Membership,* study paper from the Berkman Centre for Internet and Society   at   Harvard   Law   School,   available   at <http://www.cyber.law.harvard.edu/rcs/fish.html> (as at 28 November 2003).

[240]The Internet is a system for linking existing computer network, rather than a separate system in its own right. At its highest level coordinated by the Internet Assigned Numbers Authority (IANA) and a central Internet Registry (IR); See David R. Johnson & David G. Post, *And How Shall the Net be Governed? A Meditation on the Relative Virtues of Decentralised, Emergent Law,* draft paper at Cyberspace Law Institute Papers on Cyberspace Law, available at <http://www.cli.org/emdraft.html> (as at 28 November 2003).

[241]The Internet service providers (ISP), who provide access to the Internet, are intermediaries, though the consumer is largely unaware of their existence, as they operate behind the scenes.

Such Internet states could conceivably be used to avoid taxation liability, particularly important in an age of electronic money.[242]

Taking full advantage of the Internet requires an adequate understanding of its potential consequences, and the rigorous adoption of appropriate countermeasures, for example, against serious losses of data confidentiality, system integrity, and resource availability. This is as true for governments as it is for business and individuals. But it remains unclear whether emerging computer and communication technologies introduce fundamental differences with respect to how society and constitutions must respond, or whether there will be merely evolutionary changes. Some lawyers see a need for laws that are more clearly enforceable, and in some cases more technology-specific.[243] But this is a law-specific reaction, and is arguably not sufficiently broad. Social scientists are more likely to see many needs that transcend technology and the law.[244]

Certain specific areas of law have undoubtedly already been directly affected – such as information and personal privacy.[245] This has constitutional implications. Even taxation,[246] and government contracting

---

[242]See Stephen Bill & Arthur Kerrigan, *Practical application of European Value Added Tax to E-Commerce*, 38 GEORGIA L. REV. 71 (2003); Noel Cox, *Tax and Regulatory Avoidance Through Non-Traditional Alternatives to Tax Havens*, 9 NEW ZEALAND J. OF TAXATION L. & POLICY 305-327 (2003).

[243]Current problems of enforcement may be such that piecemeal approach is necessary; see Noel Cox, *The regulation of cyberspace and the loss of national sovereignty*, 11 INFORM. & COMMS. TECHN. L. 241-253 (2002).

[244]See also Peter G. Neumann, *Technology, laws, and society*, 37 ASSOC. FOR COMPUTING MACHINERY. COMMS. OF THE ACM 138 (1994).

[245]See Paul M. Schwartz, *Internet privacy and the State*, 32 CONNECTICUT L. REV. 815-859 (2000); Jae-Young Kim, *Deregulation reconsidered: Protecting Internet speech in the United States, Germany, and Japan*, 24 COMMS. & THE LAW 53-75 (2002).

[246]See Reuven S. Avi-Yonah, *Globalisation, Tax Competition, and the Fiscal Crisis of the Welfare State*, 113 HARV. L. REV. 1573 (2000); Noel Cox, *Tax and Regulatory Avoidance Through Non-Traditional Alternatives to Tax Havens*, 9 NEW ZEALAND J. OF TAXATION L. & POLICY 305-327 (2003); R. Palan, *Tax Havens and the Commercialisation of State Sovereignty*, 56 INTERN. ORGANISATION 151 (2002); Edward A. Morse, *State taxation of Internet commerce: something new under the sun?*, 30(4) CREIGHTON L. REV. 1113-1167 (1997); Richard Jones & Subhajit Basu, *Taxation of electronic commerce: A developing problem*, 16(1) INTERN. REV. OF L., COMPUTERS & TECHN. 35-52 (2002) [the shift from a physically orientated commercial environment to a knowledge-based electronic environment poses serious and substantial issues in relation to taxation and taxation regimes]. See also Anthony van

has been affected[247] – the former because it was open to entrepreneurs to argue that they ought not to be subject to taxation for activities which took place in a virtual world[248] – and because of assessment and collection difficulties.

Corporate nationality may have to be rethought as a consequence of the Internet,[249] as well as franchise laws,[250] all of which are based, fundamentally, on state laws. It has also been said that the Internet will be critical for the development of environmental law.[251] Meanwhile, cyberterrorism[252] remains as a potential threat, as all those who are email users will know.[253]

It is clear that, while specific laws are effected, the Internet, because of its scope for development, and its reach, is more than simply a tool, like any other telecommunications tool. It may bring about a new paradigm shift. The metaphor of the Internet as parallel to the American western frontier, a

---

Fossen, *Financial frauds and pseudo-states in the Pacific Islands*, 37 CRIME, L. & SOCIAL CHANGE 357-378 (2002) [in particular, the "dominion of Melchizedek"].

[247]See Dan McLennan, *The online revolution in government contracting*, 76 L. INSTITUTE J. 78-81 (2002).

[248]See Noel Cox, *Tax and Regulatory Avoidance Through Non-Traditional Alternatives to Tax Havens*, 9 NEW ZEALAND J. OF TAXATION L. & POLICY 305-327 (2003).

[249]See Linda A. Mabry, *Multinational corporations and U.S. technology policy: rethinking the concept of corporate nationality*, 87 GEORGETOWN L. J. 563-673 (1999).

[250]See Lane Fisher & Cheryl L. Mullin, *Franchise laws in the age of electronic communication*, 19 FRANCHISE L. J. 47-51 (1999).

[251]See Jocelyn C. Adkins, *The Internet: a critical technology for the state of environmental law*, 8 VILLANOVA ENVIRONMENTAL L. J. 341-357 (1997).

[252]See Renee M. Fishman, Kara Josephberg, Jane Linn, Jane Pollack & Jena Victoriano, *Threat of international cyberterrorism on the rise*, 14 INTELLECTUAL PROPERTY & TECHN. L. J. 23 (2002) [Riptech Inc., an Internet security firm, released its Internet Security Threat Report in July 2002, finding that international cyber-attacks against companies was steadily increasing. "Hackers" had successfully launched more than 180,000 Internet attacks against the 400 subject companies compared with approximately 160,000 attacks launched in the previous 6 months].

[253]"Spam," unsolicited email messages, constitute a growing proportion of messages received; See Jonathan Krim, *Spam's Cost To Business Escalates*, THE WASHINGTON POST, 13 March 2003, available at <http://www.washingtonpost.com/ac2/wp-dyn/A17754-2003Mar12> (as at 10 December 2003).

"place" where government should generally refrain from regulation, has been criticised as misleading people into overestimating the Internet's ability to guarantee freedom and opportunity.[254] An alternative metaphor, that of the feudal society, has been proposed.[255] This metaphor emphasises the role of law in the development of the Internet – and the mutual interdependence of users. Both may explain some aspects of the Internet, but are possibly incomplete of themselves.

The view which was common during the 1990s, of cyberspace as a place of freedom that cannot be regulated and that is more or less immune to control, has turned out to be far from correct.[256] Lawrence Lessig, who had been seen as one of the proponents of the libertarian view, has detected a trend towards more and more regulation through code under the influence of commerce regulation.[257] This would indicate that significant constitutional effects are less likely to occur. However, the nature of the Internet, the way in which it was created and operates, give important indications as to possible constitutional consequences.

At its highest level the Internet is co-ordinated by the Internet Assigned Numbers Authority (IANA) and a central Internet Registry (IR).[258] However, as might be expected of a system which has no physical home, the Internet has no controlling body, though the ICANN (Internet Corporation for Assigned Names and Numbers) regulates some aspects of the net. This is the non-profit corporation that was formed to assume responsibility for the Internet Protocol (IP) address space allocation, protocol parameter assignment, domain name system management, and root server system management functions previously performed under U.S. Government contract by the Internet Assigned Numbers Authority (IANA) and other entities.[259]

---

[254]See Alfred C. Yen, *Western frontier or feudal society?: Metaphors and Perceptions of cyberspace*, 17 BERKELEY TECHN. L. J. 1207-1263 (2002).

[255]See Alfred C. Yen, *Western frontier or feudal society?: Metaphors and Perceptions of cyberspace*, 17 BERKELEY TECHN. L. J. 1207-1263 (2002); Peter Drahos & John Braithwaite, *Information feudalism: who owns the knowledge economy?* (2003).

[256]LAWRENCE LESSIG, CODE AND OTHER LAWS OF CYBERSPACE, 5 (1999).

[257]LAWRENCE LESSIG, CODE AND OTHER LAWS OF CYBERSPACE, 61 et seq (1999).

[258]See David G. Post & David R. Johnson, *'Chaos Prevailing on Every Continent': Towards a New Theory of Decentralised Decision-Making in Complex Systems*, Social Science Research Network Electronic Library <http://papers.ssrn.com/sol3/delivery.cfm/99032613.pdf?abstractid=157 692> (as at 1 December 2003).

[259]See Kim G. von Arx, *ICANN – Now and then: ICANN's Reform and its*

No one country can alone regulate the Internet effectively, as is seen in the internationalisation of ICANN[260] – though it is possible for individual countries to exercise at least partial control the Internet within their territory.[261] For primarily technological, economic and political reasons, self-regulation by the Internet Service Providers (ISP) has been proposed as a suitable regulatory system for the Internet.[262] But it may be questioned whether self-regulation of the Internet is sufficient, particularly because of its transnational nature,[263] and because of the need for countries to regulate certain aspects of Internet use. However, there would appear to be some truth in these claims.

The limits of national control of the Internet were perhaps exaggerated.[264] Principally that is because nations are increasingly acting in concert to deal with the borderless nature of cyberspace by creating both relatively uniform laws across jurisdictions, and agreements for international co-operation in surveillance and investigation.[265] A country has no choice but to promote vigorously the introduction of new technology in order to

---

problems, DUKE L. & TECHN. REV. 7 (2003).

[260]See, for instance, James S. Fishkin, *Deliberate Polling As a Model for ICANN Membership*, 1999, Study paper from the Berkman Centre for Internet and Society at Harvard Law School, at <http://www.cyber.law.harvard.edu/rcs/fish.html> (as at 28 November 2003).

[261]See Jack Linchuan Qiu, *Virtual Censorship in China: Keeping the Gate between the Cyberspaces*, 4 INTERN. J. OF COMMS. L. & POLICY 1 (1999-2000); C. Elliott, *The Internet – A New World without frontiers*, N.Z.L.J. 405 (1998).

[262]These have limitations, such as being bound by national boundaries (they regulate behaviour of participants coming from a particular territory), lacking in efficient sanctions, public accountability and actual monitoring and reviewing systems; See Joseph A. Cannataci & Jeanne Pia Mifsud Bonnici, *Can self-regulation satisfy the transnational requisite of successful Internet regulation?*, 17(1) INTERN. REV. OF L., COMPUTERS & TECHN. 51 (2003).

[263]See Joseph A. Cannataci & Jeanne Pia Mifsud Bonnici, *Can self-regulation satisfy the transnational requisite of successful Internet regulation?*, 17(1) INTERN. REV. OF L., COMPUTERS & TECHN. 51 (2003).

[264]See Jack L. Goldsmith, *Against Cyberanarchy*, 65 U. CHICAGO L. REV. 1199-1250 (1998).

[265]See A.B. Overby, *Will cyberlaw be uniform?: an introduction to the UNCITRAL Model law on Electronic Commerce*, 7 TULANE J. OF INTERN. & COMP. L. 219-310 (1999); Graham Greenleaf, *An Endnote on Regulating Cyberspace: Architecture vs Law?*, 21 U. NEW SOUTH WALES L. J. 593 (1998), available at <http://www.austlii.edu.au/au/other/unswlj.OLD/thematic/1998/vol21n o2/greenleaf.html> (as at 1 December 2003).

maintain and increase its international competitiveness[266] – and this may mean the adoption of international norms – such as UNCITRAL, in the drafting of which it has had comparatively little influence.[267] Increasingly, private, non-state parties are regulating cyberspace.[268] The resulting uncertainty has led some to argue that law should recognise a separate jurisdiction, or even a separate sovereignty, for the Internet.[269]

As well as being a threat to sovereign authority, the Internet may allow new opportunities for an increase in surveillance[270] and authority[271] – or for an increase in public participation in government. In addition to this globalising effect, Grady argues that the Internet is affecting liberty.[272] He asserts that the traditional view has been pessimistic about information technology's probable effect on liberty.[273] His view is that the new networks, spawned by the Internet and other information technology, are hopeful developments.[274] Essentially, these break down constitutional,

---

[266]cf SHIRLEY SERAFINI & MICHEL ANDRIEU, THE INFORMATION REVOLUTION AND ITS IMPLICATIONS FOR CANADA, 96 (1981).

[267]See Kara Josephberg, Jane Pollack, Jenna Victoriano & Oriyan Gitig, *Singapore free trade agreement addresses domain names*, 15 Intellectual Property & Techn. L. J. 20 (2003).

[268]See Paul Schiff Berman, *Cyberspace and the State Action Debate: The Cultural Value of Applying Constitutional Norms to 'Private' Regulation*, 71 U. COLORADO L. REV. 1265-1266 (2000).

[269]See Jack L. Goldsmith & Lawrence Lessig, *Grounding the Virtual Magistrate*, <http://www.lessig.org/content/articles/works/magistrate.html> (as at 28 November 2003). At the very least, that it should self-regulate; David R. Johnson & David G. Post, *Law and Borders: The Rise of Law in Cyberspace*, 48 STANFORD L. REV. 1367 (1996).

[270]See Graham Greenleaf, *An Endnote on Regulating Cyberspace: Architecture vs Law?*, 21 U. NEW SOUTH WALES L. J. 593 (1998), available at <http://www.austlii.edu.au/au/other/unswlj.OLD/thematic/1998/vol21n o2/greenleaf.html> (as at 1 December 2003).

[271]See, for instance, Jack Linchuan Qiu, *Virtual Censorship in China: Keeping the Gate between the Cyberspaces*, 4 INTERN. J. OF COMMS. L. & POLICY 1 (1999/2000).

[272]See Mark F. Grady, *The state and the networked economy*, 25 HARV. J. OF L. & PUBL. POLICY 15 (2001).

[273]He cites the novels 1984 (GEORGE ORWELL, 1949), and BRAVE NEW WORLD (ALDOUS HUXLEY, 1932). Pessimism is not, of course, limited to predictions concerning the Internet – an informal pre-millennial survey of world leaders and Nobel laureates garnered generally pessimistic predictions across a range of fields; See Leonard M. Salter, *Predictions for the Next Millennium*, 42 ORANGE COUNTY LAWYER 16 (2000).

governmental and administrative barriers. This is a libertarians dream.

As well as possibly leading to increased liberty,[275] the Internet may potentially also improve the quality of development in less developed countries, through increased political participation and communication.[276] Kalir has also noted the trend towards democratisation in the 1990s,[277] though whether it can be said to be seen as a defining phenomenon of globalisation[278] may perhaps be doubted. Globalisation can itself also be a tool against corruption.[279] Certainly greater exposure through improved communications, and increased expectations brought about by globalisation, have raised awareness of different political, social and economic norms.

Sunstein has argued that, by increasing the possibility of community, the Internet has undermined the American republic.[280] In his view, the printing press helped create modern nationalism, as books and newspapers came to be written in the vernacular, encouraging a conception of a shared community among groups of people who would never actually meet. His concern is that through the Internet we may choose to find only "echo chambers" of our own opinions, magnifying and confirming our inclinations and resulting in a deeply polarised society.[281] This is Grady's liberty carried to extremes.[282] It has been countered with the obvious but

---

[274]See Mark F. Grady, *The state and the networked economy*, 25 HARV. J. OF L. & PUBL. POLICY 15 (2001).

[275]See Mark F. Grady, *The state and the networked economy*, 25 HARV. J. OF L. & PUBL. POLICY 15-29 (2001).

[276]See WILLIAM J. STOVER, INFORMATION TECHNOLOGY IN THE THIRD WORLD: CAN I.T. LEAD TO HUMANE NATIONAL DEVELOPMENT? (1984).

[277]Doron M. Kalir, *Taking Globalisation Seriously: Towards General Jurisprudence*, 39 COLUMBIA J. OF TRANSNATIONAL L. 785, 816 (2001).

[278]Doron M. Kalir, *Taking Globalisation Seriously: Towards General Jurisprudence*, 39 COLUMBIA J. OF TRANSNATIONAL L. 785, 816 (2001).

[279]Africa is the only continent none of whose states have joined the conventions against international bribery, and very few African states have national laws attempting to fill the gap. The Internet and other new technologies are developing as parallel, mostly non-governmental tools against corruption. Unlike transnational and most national laws, their impact has already been clearly visible in Africa and they offer at least the possibility of substantial interference with corruption in the short to medium term; See Peter W. Schroth & Preeti Sharma, *Transnational law and technology as potential forces against corruption in Africa*, 41 MANAGEMENT DECISION 296 (2003).

[280]See CASS R. SUNSTEIN, REPUBLIC.COM (2001).

[281]See CASS R. SUNSTEIN, REPUBLIC.COM (2001).

important critique that cyberspace in fact also functions in exactly the opposite way – it allows us to discover the new, to learn about the unfamiliar, to begin to understand one another.[283] What may be different about the Internet is not its function, but its breadth and scope. It is truly global,[284] or as global as anything can be in a largely heterogeneous world.

It should come as no surprise then that an emerging international law dimension of the Internet has been identified.[285] The reach of the Internet is global, and therefore its legal implications are global. If the Internet is to continue to function effectively it will be necessary to strengthen the architecture or code through which it operates,[286] but international law is also a means for preventing this from being captured by powerful private vested interests or by countries more advanced in computer technology.[287] There is evidence that this latter may be already happening. The 2003 draft free-trade agreement between the U.S. and Singapore included a requirement that both countries participate in the ICANN Government Advisory Committee, the group that manages the Internet's domain name system. This involved adopting policies similar to ones created by ICANN,[288]

---

[282]See Mark F. Grady, *The state and the networked economy*, 25 HARV. J. OF L. & PUBL. POLICY 15 (2001).

[283]See Anupam Chander, *Whose Republic?*, 69 THE U. CHICAGO L. REV. 1479-150 (2002)0.

[284]See *Global Internet Statistics*, Global Reach, available at <http://www.glreach.com/globstats/> (as at 10 December 2003).

[285]See Franz C. Mayer, *The Internet and Public International Law – Worlds Apart?*, 12 EUROPEAN J. OF INTERN. LAW 617-622 (2001); Ruth Wedgwood, *The Internet and Public Intern. Law: Cyber-Nations*, 88 KENTUCKY L. J. 957 (2000); KLAUS W. GREWLICH, GOVERNANCE IN 'CYBERSPACE' – ACCESS AND PUBLIC INTEREST IN GLOBAL TELECOMMUNICATIONS (1999); MAKOTO IBUSUKI (ed), TRANSNATIONAL CYBERSPACE LAW (2000) [Grewlich and Ibusuki focus on economic transnational aspects].

[286]In particular, see LAWRENCE LESSIG, CODE AND OTHER LAWS OF CYBERSPACE (1999) [For Lessig the "code" of cyberspace means it architectural combination of software and hardware. For him this was its most significant body of law, one which transcended the strictures of ordinary law].

[287]Franz C. Mayer, *The Internet and Public International Law – Worlds Apart?*, 12 EUROPEAN J. OF INTERN. L. 617, 621-622 (2001). Contemporary international law envisions a pluralist world in which communities may preserve their cultural and religious diversity; L. ALI KHAN, THE EXTINCTION OF NATION-STATES: A WORLD WITHOUT BORDERS, 3 (1996).

[288]The Internet Corporation for Assigned Names and Numbers (ICANN)

which is a US-based incorporation, subject to U.S. laws.[289] The US's response to disputes over domain names (the Anticybersquatting Consumer Protection Act (ACPA)[290]) permits a trademark owner to seek cancellation or transfer of the domain name itself, thereby expanding the scope of the ACPA to encompass disputes with little direct connection to the US.[291] It is perhaps inevitable that the U.S. should be in this position, given its dominant Internet presence. However, it is clearly unsatisfactory to have one country, however benign, dictate terms to others.

One possible solution is to draw from current economic regulation examples. The World Trade Organisation (WTO) governance arrangements have traditionally reflected the interests of producers channelled through government trade negotiators. Abbott has argued that the producer-driven governance model is not suited to the highly integrated international society of the twenty-first century. He argues that the WTO governance structure should be adapted to account for more diverse interests, including those of marginalised developing countries, non-governmental organisations (NGOs), and individuals.[292] This view has also been advanced by McGinnis,[293]

---

regulates some aspects of the net. This is the non-profit corporation that was formed to assume responsibility for the Internet Protocol (IP) address space allocation, protocol parameter assignment, domain name system management, and root server system management functions previously performed under U.S. Government contract by Internet Assigned Numbers Authority (IANA) and other entities. That no single country can regulate the Internet is seen in the internationalisation of ICANN. See for instance, James S. Fishkin, *Deliberate Polling As a Model for ICANN Membership*, study paper from the Berkman Centre for Internet and Society at Harvard Law School, available at <http://www.cyber.law.harvard.edu/rcs/fish.html> (as at 28 November 2003).

[289]See Kara Josephberg, Jane Pollack, Jenna Victoriano & Oriyan Gitig, *Singapore free trade agreement addresses domain names*, 15 INTELLECTUAL PROPERTY & TECHN. L. J. 20 (2003).

[290]In § 1000(a)(9) of Pub. L. No. 106-113 (Nov. 29, 1999), and published as title III, § 3001 et seq., in Appendix I of that law.

[291]See Catherine T. Struve & R. Polk Wagner, *Realspace sovereigns in cyberspace: Problems with the Anticybersquatting Consumer Protection Act*, 17 BERKELEY TECHN. L. J. 989-1041 (2002).

[292]See Frederick M. Abbott, *Distributed governance at the WTO-WIPO: An evolving model for open-architecture integrated governance*, 3 J. OF INTERN. ECONOMIC L. 63 (2000).

[293]John O. McGinnis, *The Symbiosis of Constitutionalism and Technology*, 25 HARV. J. OF L. & PUBL. POLICY 3, 9 (2001); John O. McGinnis & Mark L. Movsesian, *The World Trade Constitution*, 114 HARV. L. REV. 511, 514-515

who envisages the prospect of international federalism through the WTO and other global economic organisation.[294] But he also foresees such international federalism collapsing for much the same reason that he saw U.S. federalism decline – a tendency to centralisation at the expense of the states.[295]

Both Lessig[296] and Vaidhyanathan[297] are concerned about the future of creativity in an increasingly propertised world, leading them to conclude that the world is faced with a crucial choice regarding the future of the Internet. This is not a choice which is cast along ideological or political lines, but rather a choice between old and new conceptions of legal regulation, property, and creativity.[298] This raises constitutional issues – concerns about the role of the state in the economy and society. Nor can we be sure whether regulation of the Internet is impeding commerce, or aiding it.[299] The Napster case has been seen as a symbol heavy with political overtones about the future of the relationship between innovation and law in a high technology world.[300]

We can see a range of tensions, between countries, and within

---

(2000).

[294]John O. McGinnis, *The Symbiosis of Constitutionalism and Technology*, 25 HARV. J. OF L. & PUBL. POLICY 3, 9-10 (2001).

[295]John O. McGinnis, *The Symbiosis of Constitutionalism and Technology*, 25 HARV. J. OF L. & PUBL. POLICY 3, 10 (2001). However, due to the much greater complexity of a world federalism, this process would be much slower than the American prototype; John O. McGinnis & Mark L. Movsesian, *The World Trade Constitution*, 114 HARV. L. REV. 511, 543-544 (2000).

[296]See LAWRENCE LESSIG, THE FUTURE OF IDEAS: THE FATE OF THE COMMONS IN A CONNECTED WORLD (2001).

[297]See SIVA VAIDHYANATHAN, COPYRIGHT AND COPYWRONGS: THE RISE OF INTELLECTUAL PROPERTY AND HOW IT THREATENS CREATIVITY (2001).

[298]See Sonia K. Katyal, *Ending the revolution*, 80 TEXAS L. REV. 1465-148 (2002).

[299]See John C. Williams, *The role of the U.S. government in encouraging technological innovation*, 15 CANADA-U.S. L. J. 219-228 (1989); Robert G. BlacK.B.urn, *The role of the Canadian government in encouraging innovations*, 15 CANADA-U.S. L. J. 229-236 (1989). For a more specific example, see Derek E. Empie, *The dormant Internet: are state regulators of motor vehicle sales by manufacturers on the Information Superhighway obstructing interstate and Internet commerce?*, 18 GEORGIA ST. UNIV. L. Rev. 827-857 (2002).

[300]See Sonia K. Katyal, *Ending the revolution*, 80(6) TEXAS L. REV. 1465-1486 (2002).

countries, including between states where there is a federal constitution. It is not yet clear what the long-term effects of the Internet will be, but so far we see a tendency to centralisation (including usurpation of regulation by federal government),[301] and increased international co-operation (as for UNCITRAL). This latter is particularly apparent in the field of international commerce.

(b) (i) The Internet and commerce

The Internet has a particularly important impact upon commerce, especially business to consumer commerce.[302] It is altering the nature of global trade, in ways of which we can only guess at. But the analogy between the rise of a separate law of cyberspace and the Law Merchant – the international legal rules and procedures which regulated commerce for centuries – has been observed.[303] This analogy may give us some guidance to the possible constitutional implications of the Internet.

Commerce has rarely if ever been exclusively national. Throughout the course of human history the practical realities of international trade meant that much business was conducted at a distance, often overseas, with only limited opportunities for face-to-face contact between merchants.[304] Many transactions were conducted by agents, whilst many relied upon correspondence. In Europe, and those countries which derived their legal traditions from that continent, each form of trade was regulated by rules of private international law, including the custom and usages of the merchants, the Law Merchant, or *lex mercatoria*.[305] Gerard de Malynes regarded Law Merchant as customary law approved by the authority of all kingdoms and not as law established by the sovereignty of any prince.[306] It was the "law of

---

[301]John O. McGinnis, *The Symbiosis of Constitutionalism and Technology*, 25 HARV. J. OF L. & PUBL. POLICY 3, 8 (2001).

[302]"B2C." It greatly increases the scope for international trade by private persons, with the resulting regulatory problems, particularly difficulties of dispute resolution, and enforcement.

[303]See I. Trotter Hardy, *The Proper Legal Regime for 'Cyberspace'*, 55 U. PITTSBURGH L. REV. 993, 1020 (1994); Noel Cox, *The Regulation of Cyberspace and the Loss of National Sovereignty*, 11 INFORM. & COMMUN. TECHN. L. 241 (2002).

[304]This remained true in more recent times; See Michael B. Miller, *The business trip: Maritime networks in the twentieth century*, 77 BUSINESS HISTORY REV. 1 (2003).

[305]See LEON TRAKMAN, THE LAW MERCHANT – THE EVOLUTION OF COMMERCIAL LAW (1983).

all nations."[307] Certain elements of the modern commercial law grew out of the Law Merchant,[308] which indeed continues to develop today as customary private international law.[309] Custom is general state practice accepted as law.[310] The elements of custom are a generalised repetition of similar acts by competent state authorities and a sentiment that such acts are juridically necessary to maintain and develop international relations.[311]

The law merchant evolved over a relatively long period of time, so that no particular country or era could be said to have had an excessive influence on its development.[312] The process was largely evolutionary and, in so far as it was not imposed by a single sovereign state, was democratic.[313] It was largely created by the merchants themselvs,[314] though subject to

---

[306]See GERARD DE MALYNES, CONSUETUDO VEL LEX MERCATORIA, OR THE ANCIENT LAW MERCHANT (1979).

[307]*Luke v. Lyde*, 2 Burr 882; 97 ER 614 (1759), per Lord Mansfield, C.J.

[308]See LEON TRAKMAN, THE LAW MERCHANT – THE EVOLUTION OF COMMERCIAL LAW (1983); Bruce Benson, *The Spontaneous Evolution of Commercial Law*, 55 SOUTHERN ECONOMIC J. 644, 646-647 (1989).

[309]See KLAUS PETER BERGER, THE CREEPING CODIFICATION OF LEX MERCATORIA (1999).

[310]*Lotus Case (France v. Turkey)*, 1927 P.C.I.J. ser. A. No. 10 (Judgment of 7 September 1927), *Asylum Case (Colombia v. Peru)*, 1950 I.C.J. 266, 276 (Judgment of 20 November 1950), *Delimitation of the Maritime Boundary in the Gulf of Maine Area (Canada v. U.S.)*, 1950 I.C.J. 266, 299-300 (Judgment of 12 October 1950), *Fisheries Case (U.K. v. Norway)*, 1951 I.C.J. 116 (Judgment of 18 December 1951), *North Sea Continental Shelf Cases (Federal Republic of Germany v. Denmark; Federal Republic of Germany v. The Netherlands)*, 1969 I.C.J. 3, 43-45 (Judgment of 20 February 1969), and *Military and Paramilitary Activities in and against Nicaragua (Nicaragua v. U.S.)*, 1969 I.C.J. 3, 97-98 (Judgment of 27 June 1969).

[311]*North Sea Continental Shelf Cases (Federal Republic of Germany v. Denmark; Federal Republic of Germany v. The Netherlands)*, 1969 I.C.J. 3, 44-45 (Judgment of 20 February 1969). The International Court of Justice emphasised the importance of opinio juris even in the face of inconsistent state practice in *Military and Paramilitary Activities in and against Nicaragua (Nicaragua v. U.S.)*, Merits 1986 I.C.J. 14 (Judgment of 27 June 1986). Opinio juris may be determined from resolutions of international organisations, notably the General Assembly.

[312]See Oliver Volckart & Antje Mangels, *Are the roots of the modern lex mercatoria really mediæval?*, 65(3) SOUTHERN ECONOMIC J. 427 (1999).

[313]"Mercocratic" would perhaps be a more accurate term.

[314]See LEON TRAKMAN, THE LAW MERCHANT – THE EVOLUTION OF COMMERCIAL LAW (1983).

alteration by individual states.[315] This latter process became more pronounced – particularly during the eighteenth and nineteenth centuries[316] – but the law merchant remains a supra-national law.[317] It may be that the same will be said of the Internet, when its definitive history is written.[318]

The almost instantaneous global reach of the Internet, and the potentially adverse affects of the Internet on countries – particularly in economic and social terms – combine to ensure that governments have responded to the challenge of this emerging technology. But they have not responded consistently.

Unlike the *lex mercatoria*, which developed over an extended period of time, just as customary international law has traditionally developed,[319] the growth of the Internet may not permit the international community the luxury of time to develop customary rules. For this reason states may have little choice but to defer to the views of the majority, or the stronger economic blocks, whatever implications that may have for the longer-term future of state sovereignty, and for domestic laws.[320]

The approaches of states vary, as might be expected. In its broad approach to the Internet, the U.S. has chosen to rely on self-regulation,[321] rather than direct regulation. This is subject to increasingly important exceptions, however, such with respect to Internet pornography,[322] and national security.[323] The Federal Trade Commission (FTC) has also been

---

[315]See *The Antelope*, 10 Wheat. 66 (1825), per Marshall C.J.

[316]See S. Todd Lowry, *Lord Mansfield and the Law Merchant: Law and Economics in the Eighteenth Century*, 7 J. OF ECONOMIC ISSUES 605 (1973).

[317]Robert D. Cooter, *Structural adjudication and the new law merchant: A model of decentralised law*, 12 INTERN. REV. OF L. & ECONOMICS 215 (1994).

[318]If such a thing ever comes to pass.

[319]See W.P. HEERE & J.P.S. OFFERHAUS, INTERNATIONAL LAW IN HISTORICAL PERSPECTIVE (1998).

[320]See, for instance, the situation of Singapore, in its negotiations with the US; Kara Josephberg, Jane Pollack, Jenna Victoriano & Oriyan Gitig, *Singapore free trade agreement addresses domain names*, 15(6) INTELLECTUAL PROPERTY & TECHN. L. J. 20 (2003).

[321]See The White House, *A Framework for Global Electronic Commerce*, 1997, at <http://www.technology.gov/digeconomy/framewrk.htm> (as at 28 November 2003).

[322]Children's Online Protection Act, 1998, Pub. L. No. 105-277, Div C, tit. 13, ch 1302(6) available at <http://www.cdt.org/legislation/105th/speech/copa.html> (as at 28 November 2003). States may even resort to the use of force in cyberspace; Dimitrios Delibasis, *The right to use force in cyberspace: Defining the rules of engagement*, 11(3) FEATURE 255-268 (2002).

seeking a more active role in regard to spammers.[324] An alternative approach to that of self-regulation is a balance of self-regulation and direct regulation, as advocated by the European Union.[325] A third option would be direct regulation, which also has support, as in China.[326] Thus far there has however been little sign of a global consensus developing as to the appropriate form of Internet regulation, domestic, trans-national, or international. This presents major problems for the consumer of goods and services sold via the Internet, in particular.

It also has implications for constitutions. For legislation is no longer overwhelmingly domestic in origin, even though it may still be enacted by domestic legislative bodies,[327] due to an increasing number of treaties and conventions. Some legislative provisions have been made to accommodate this new grundnorm of the globalisation of electronic commerce.[328] If

---

[323]See, for instance, the USA Patriot Act of 2001, Public Law 107-56.

[324]The FTC uses the unsolicited emails stored in its database to pursue law enforcement actions against people who send deceptive spam email; *You've Got Spam: How to "Can" Unwanted Email,* <http://www3.ftc.gov/bcp/conline/pubs/online/inbox.htm> (as at 1 December 2003). The FTC enters Internet, telemarketing, identity theft and other fraud-related complaints into CONSUMER SENTINEL at <http://www.consumer.gov/sentinel/> (as at 1 December 2003), a secure, online database available to hundreds of civil and criminal law enforcement agencies in the U.S. and abroad.

[325]Common Position Adopted by the Council with a View to the Adoption of a Directive of the European Parliament and the Council on Certain Legal Aspects of Information Society Services, in Particular Electronic Commerce, in the Internal Market 14263/1/99 REV (February 28, 2000) ("Electronic Commerce Directive"). See now "Electronic Commerce" Directive 2000/31/EC OJ 2000 L178/1.

[326]See Jack Linchuan Qiu, *Virtual Censorship in China: Keeping the Gate between the Cyberspaces,* 4 INTERN. J. OF COMMS. L. & POLICY 1 (1999-2000); Renee M. Fishman, Kara Josephberg, Jane Linn, Jane Pollack & Jena Victoriano, *China issues rules on content enforcement,* 14 INTELLECTUAL PROPERTY & TECHN. L. J. 24 (2002). China has regulated access to the Internet through centralised filtered servers, and by requiring filters for in-state Internet service providers and end-users; Timothy Wu, *Cyberspace Sovereignty? – The Internet and the International System,* 10 HARV. J. OF L. & TECHN. 647, 652-654 (1997).

[327]Unless, of course, they have relinquished legislative authority, in part or whole, as have members of the European Union. See TREVOR C. HARTLEY, CONSTITUTIONAL PROBLEMS OF THE EUROPEAN UNION (1999).

commerce is now seen to be primarily international in nature, the role of domestic law is restricted. The limitations of paper-based evidential requirements when faced with the requirements of modern electronic communications, are a case in point. The United Nations Commission on International Trade Law (UNCITRAL) Model Law on Electronic Commerce provides that an electronic signature may be legally effective as a manual signature, but does not define an electronic signature.[329] Thus although international treaties or conventions may give some guidance, it remains for the domestic legislature to provide the detail.

As an example, the Electronic Transactions Act 2000 (NZ) is based on work carried out by the New Zealand Law Commission, and closely follows both the Model Law on Electronic Commerce prepared by UNCITRAL in 1996 and the Australian Electronic Transactions Act 1999 (Cth) – itself heavily influenced by UNCITRAL.[330] The purpose of the Act is to facilitate the use of electronic technology. This it does by reducing uncertainty regarding the legal effect of electronic communications, and allows certain paper-based legal requirements to be met by using functionally equivalent electronic technology.[331]

The Act is predicated upon the idea that the principles applicable to the making of a contract by electronic means should be no different to the principles applicable to contracts formed orally or in writing on paper. Indeed, the decided cases appear to have accepted that proposition as self-evident.[332] These principles may vary from country to country, though there are certain points upon which all jurisdictions agree.

It is these common elements which form the basis for the United Nations Commission on International Trade (UNCITRAL) Model Law on

---

[328]In Kelsen's philosophy of law, a grundnorm is the basic, fundamental postulate, which justifies all principles and rules of the legal system and which all inferior rules of the system may be deduced; See MICHAEL HAYBACK, CARL SCHMITT AND HANS KELSEN IN THE CRISIS OF DEMOCRACY BETWEEN WORLD WARS I AND II, Universitaet Salzburg DrIur thesis (1990).

[329]Art 7.

[330]See J.D. Gregory, *The authentication of digital records*, 6 EDI L. REV.: LEGAL ASPECTS OF PAPERLESS COMMUNICATION 47-63 (1999); J.D. Gregory, *Solving legal issues in electronic commerce*, 32 CANADIAN BUSINESS L. J. 84-131 (1999).

[331]See EXPLANATORY NOTE TO ELECTRONIC TRANSACTIONS BILL.

[332]*Databank Systems Ltd v. Commissioner of Inland Revenue*, 3 N.Z.L.R. 385 (1990) (Privy Council); *Corinthian Pharmaceutical Systems Inc v. Lederle Laboratories*, 724 F Supp 605 (1989); NEW ZEALAND LAW COMMISSION, ELECTRONIC COMMERCE PART ONE, para 52 (1998).

Electronic Commerce. Under article 7 of the Model Law, the elements of the functional equivalent to a signature are the need:

- To identify the person and to indicate that person's approval of the information contained in the data message; and

- For the method to be as reliable as was appropriate for the purpose for which the message was generated or communicated.[333]

Article 7 only applies where a signature is a requirement of law. Where a signature is not required by law then the normal rules in relation to proving an agreement apply. These general rules allow some flexibility to domestic law. But they also impose some common standards.

Whilst it is not unusual for domestic laws to be influenced by international developments, it is perhaps true that New Zealand – and most other countries – had little choice but to adopt the UNCITRAL model, and alter its domestic laws accordingly.[334] The nature of electronic commerce has some important differences from traditional trade, not least of which is its speed and universality. This latter attribute means that the electronic age poses particular problems for municipal legal systems, and for the states which created them.

Although there was an important international law element, all law was – and is – prima facie territorial in nature.[335] But many international laws were recognised by national legal systems, just as the laws of war involved both domestic and international elements.[336] In the English experience,

---

[333]NEW ZEALAND LAW COMMISSION, ELECTRONIC COMMERCE PART ONE, paras 316-320, 344-345 (1998).

[334]See also Singapore; Kara Josephberg, Jane Pollack, Jenna Victoriano & Oriyan Gitig, *Singapore free trade agreement addresses domain names*, 15 Intellectual Property & Techn. L. J. 20 (2003).

[335]*American Banana Co v. United Fruit Co*, 213 U.S. 347, 357 (1909). Recognising the problems of extraterritorial enforcement, the U.S. Supreme Court has held that "legislation of Congress, unless a contrary intent appears, is merely to apply only within the territorial jurisdiction of the United States." *EEOC v. Arabian American Oil Co*, 499 U.S. 244, 248 (1991), citing *Foley Bros Inc v. Filardo*, 336 U.S. 281, 285 (1949). Although Congress "has the authority to enforce its laws beyond [US] boundaries," this principle "serves to protect against unintended clashes between our laws and those of other nations, which could result in international discord." EEOC, 499 U.S. at 248, citing *McCulloch v. Sociedad Nacional de Marineros de Honduras*, 372 U.S. 10, 20-22 (1963).

[336]See ADAM ROBERTS & RICHARD GUELLF (eds), LAWS OF WAR (2000);

which was to largely shape the laws of the common law world, these international laws were recognised by the common law, albeit often at the instigation of Parliament.[337] Although the substantive law and procedures of the common law world broadly reflected the international character of trade, it was also influenced by the insular tendencies of domestic law.[338] This was scarcely surprising since it was administered in national courts, imbued with the approach of a national legal system.[339] Sometimes the domestic influences prevailed, and the law was but little affected by international developments.[340] At other times international developments had a great influence on domestic laws.[341] In part this depended upon the contemporary strength of the individual nation-state, or upon its size and international influence.[342]

The advent of modern electronic trade conducted through the Internet, and the consequent challenges to territorial borders, combined with the growth in regional free-trade alliances, has meant that there is an increased emphasis upon the international aspects of law.[343] But though the number of international treaties and conventions has increased,[344] this is only partly a consequence of technological change. Globalisation, for

---

GEOFFREY BEST, HUMANITY IN WARFARE: THE MODERN HISTORY OF THE INTERNATIONAL LAW OF ARMED CONFLICT (1980).

[337]As with the Statute of the Staple 1352-3 (27 Edw. III stat. 2) (Eng.).

[338]See Noel Cox, *The regulation of cyberspace and the loss of national sovereignty*, 11 INFORM. & COMMS. TECHN. L. 241-253 (2002).

[339]See David R. Johnson, & David G. Post, *Law and Borders: The Rise of Law in Cyberspace*, 48 STANFORD L. REV. 1367 (1996).

[340]As in the commercial law of England from the late nineteenth century to the late twentieth century; see ALAN HARDING, A SOCIAL HISTORY OF ENGLISH LAW (1966).

[341]Particularly from within the same legal tradition, see, for example, JEROME ELKIND (ed), THE IMPACT OF AMERICAN LAW ON ENGLISH AND COMMONWEALTH LAW: A BOOK OF ESSAYS (1978).

[342]See RODERICK FLOUD & DONALD MCCLOSKEY, THE ECONOMIC HISTORY OF BRITAIN SINCE 1700 (2d ed. 1994).

[343]For one small aspect of this see Ben Boer, *The Globalisation of Environmental Law: The Role of the United Nations*, 20 MELBOURNE UNIV. L. REV. 101-125 (1995).

[344]See for example, J. Clift, *The UNCITRAL Model Law and electronic equivalents to traditional bills of lading*, 27 J. OF THE SECTION ON BUSINESS L. OF THE INTERN. BAR ASSOC. 311-317 (1999); S. Eiselen, *Electronic commerce and the United Nations Convention on Contracts for the International Sale of Goods (CISG) 1980*, 6 EDI L. REV.: LEGAL ASPECTS OF PAPERLESS COMMUNICATION 21-46 (1999).

political and economic reasons, continues to have widespread effects on law. Nor is the Internet, as a challenge to the legal system, a novel phenomenon.[345] Domestic legal systems have faced before the challenge of accommodating other legal traditions and technological changes.[346] What may be different now is the extent to which the changes which this new technology brings are being decided at international and supranational level, and this has important implications for national sovereignty and independence.[347] Indeed, it has been said that the view that the nation-state alone should monopolise international affairs in an increasingly inadequate proposition.[348]

The literature on the jurisdictional challenges of e-commerce is voluminous, and is largely focussed on private law aspects of this issue, namely whose courts and whose laws will apply in relation to private disputes arising out of e-commerce.[349] These rules are those of private international law, or the rules of conflict of laws. The fundamental question, in any legal dispute, is in which country's legal system will the dispute be resolved? This is the forum question, and concerns the jurisdiction.[350] Secondly, whose law will apply to the transaction? This is the choice of law question – the proper or applicable law.[351] Thirdly, there is the question of

---

[345]See Jack L. Goldsmith, *Regulation of the Internet: Three Persistent Fallacies*, 73 CHICAGO-KENT L. REV. 1119-1131 (1998).

[346]See Goldsmith for a criticism of the "regulation sceptics", who (using descriptive and normative claims) assert that the Internet is fundamentally different to earlier situations, and requires unique means of regulation; Jack L. Goldsmith, *Against Cyberanarchy*, 65 U. CHICAGO L. REV. 1199-1250 (1998).

[347]See, for example, Noel Cox, *The regulation of cyberspace and the loss of national sovereignty*, 11 INFORM. & COMMS. TECHN. L. 241-253 (2002).

[348]Louis Henkin, *That S. Words: Sovereignty, and Globalisation, and Human Rights, Et Cetera*, 68 FORD L. REV. 1, 6-7 (1999).

[349]See Roger Tassé & Maxime Faille, *Online Consumer Protection in Canada: The Problem of Regulatory Jurisdiction*, 2 INTERNET & E-COMMERCE LAW IN CANADA 41 (2000-01); RONALD DE BRUIN, CONSUMER TRUST IN ELECTRONIC COMMERCE: TIME FOR BEST PRACTICE (2002); Jack L. Goldsmith, *Regulation of the Internet: Three Persistent Fallacies*, 73 CHICAGO-KENT L. REV. 1119-1131 (1998); Tapio Puurunen, *The Legislative Jurisdiction of States over Transactions in International Electronic Commerce*, 18 MARSHAL J. OF COMPUTER & INFORM. L. 689 (2000).

[350]See Franco Ferrari, *'Forum shopping' despite international uniform contract law conventions*, 51 INTERN. & COMP. L. QUARTERLY 689-707 (2002); Ralph U. Whitten, *U.S. conflict-of-laws doctrine and forum shopping, international and domestic (revisited)*, 37 TEXAS INTERN. L. J. 559-589 (2002).

the recognition and enforcement of judgements.[352] In the absence of evidence that foreign law applies, courts have traditionally applied the substantive and procedural rules of the forum.[353]

These rules have developed over time, and have been influenced by international conventions, such as the Hague,[354] Brussels and Lugano (for the European Union),[355] and Rome Conventions.[356] But each country has

---

[351]Substantive foreign law will apply, generally, where the parties have included a choice of law provision in a contract; where under the forum's own laws status is determined under the laws of the place of birth or marriage; in tort, where lex loci delicti applies; and in the enforcement of foreign judgments (assuming that the application of foreign law does not offend public order); See Ogilvy Renault, *Jurisdiction and the Internet: Are the traditional rules enough?*, paper prepared by the Uniform Law Conference of Canada, 1998, available at <http://www.law.ualberta.ca/alri/ulc/current/ejurisd.htm> (as at 1 December 2003), n7.

[352]In New Zealand this is governed by the Reciprocal Enforcement of Judgments Act 1934 (NZ). This has been applied to Orders in Council have been made in respect of the following countries and states: Australia (S.R. 1987/22), Australian Capital Territory (S.R. 1955/108), Basutoland (Lesotho) (S.R. 1940/88), Bechuanaland (Botswana) (S.R. 1940/88), Belgium (S.R. 1938/177), Cameroons (S.R. 1957/43), Ceylon (Sri Lanka) (S.R. 1958/23), Fiji (S.R. 1940/88), France (S.R. 1938/176), Gilbert and Ellice Islands (Kiribati) (S.R. 1940/88), Hong Kong (S.R. 1957/263), India (S.R. 1957/219), Malaya (Malaysia) (S.R. 1951/12), New South Wales (S.R. 1940/88), Nigeria (S.R. 1957/43), Norfolk Island (S.R. 1940/88), North Borneo (Sabah) (S.R. 1954/5), Northern Territory of Australia (S.R. 1957/264), Pakistan (S.R. 1958/117), Papua New Guinea (S.R. 1956/79), Queensland (S.R. 1940/88), Sarawak (S.R. 1951/12), Singapore (S.R. 1951/12), Solomon Islands (Tuvalu) (S.R. 1940/88), South Australia (S.R. 1940/88), Swaziland (S.R. 1940/88), Tasmania (S.R. 1940/306), Tonga (S.R. 1988/215), Victoria (S.R. 1940/88), Western Australia (S.R. 1940/88), and Western Samoa (S.R. 1971/124).

[353]See Franco Ferrari, *'Forum shopping' despite international uniform contract law conventions*, 51 INTERN. & COMP. L. QUARTERLY 689-707 (2002); Ralph U. Whitten, *U.S. conflict-of-laws doctrine and forum shopping, international and domestic (revisited)*, 37 TEXAS INTERN. L. J. 559-589 (2002).

[354]Convention on the Law Applicable to Contracts for the International Sale of Goods, The Hague Convention, 15 June 1955.

[355]Convention on Jurisdiction and the Enforcement of Judgments in Civil and Commercial matters, Brussels, 27 September 1968; Convention on Jurisdiction and the Enforcement of Judgments in Civil and Commercial

its own conflict of laws rules,[357] and there is no effective or established customary international law that regulates personal jurisdiction[358] – despite the failed attempt to introduce a Hague Convention on International Jurisdiction and Foreign Judgments in Civil and Commercial Matters.[359] The position in New Zealand is that the courts will have jurisdiction if documents initiating proceedings may properly be served on that court.[360] The U.S. position is that even if a foreign court passes a judgment or direction against a legal entity of a particular country say Country A, then that judgment or direction would not be applicable automatically to country A's legal entity or citizen.[361] Since 1995 there has been a great increase in the amount of cyberspace litigation, especially in the US. Some courts have simply applied traditional jurisdictional rules,[362] while others have tried to devise new tests to accommodate the peculiarity of the medium.[363] This has caused uncertainty and difficulties for courts. But the precise nature of cyber-law remains uncertain. Is it primarily national law, or a mixture of national and international? Or is it (as some have suggested) altogether different?[364]

---

matters, Lugano, 16 September 1988.

[356]Convention on the law applicable to contractual obligations, Rome, 19 June 1980.

[357]NEW ZEALAND LAW COMMISSION OF NEW ZEALAND, ELECTRONIC COMMERCE PART TWO: A BASIC LEGAL FRAMEWORK, paras 12-21 (1999).

[358]Friedrich Juenger, *Judicial Jurisdiction in the United States and in the European Communities: A Comparison*, 82 MICHIGAN L. REV. 1195, 1211 (1984).

[359]See, the *Report on the Second Meeting of the Informal Working Group on the Judgments Project*, 6-9 January 2003 (February 2003). This failed largely due to U.S. opposition, grounded in concerns that it would hinder the development of the Internet.

[360]*Cockburn v. Kinzie Industries Inc*, 1 P.R.N.Z. 243, 246 (1998) per Hardie Boys J. (HC); *Biddulph v. Wyeth Australia Pty Ltd*, 3 N.Z.L.R. 49 (1994).

[361]*Yahoo! Inc v. La Ligue contre Le Racisme et L'Antisemitisme*, 145 F. Supp. 2d 1168; 169 F. Supp. 2d 1181 (2001); Andreas Manolopoulos, *Raising 'Cyber-Borders': The Interaction Between Law and Technology*, 11(1) INTERN. J. OF L. & INFORM. TECHN. 40-58 (2003).

[362]I.e. *Bensusan Restaurant Corp v. King*, 40 USPQ (2d) 1519 (SDNY), confirmed by U.S. Court of Appeals (2d cir) 10 September 1997.

[363]See Ogilvy Renault, *Jurisdiction and the Internet: Are the traditional rules enough?*, paper prepared by the Uniform Law Conference of Canada, 1998, available at <http://www.law.ualberta.ca/alri/ulc/current/ejurisd.htm> (as at 1 December 2003).

[364]See Jack L. Goldsmith & Lawrence Lessig, *Grounding the Virtual Magistrate*, at <http://www.lessig.org/content/articles/works/magistrate.html> (as at

These are important questions, for the effective enforcement of consumer laws will only be possible if these can be answered, as there are limitations to what can be achieved through international co-operation alone. If enforcement remains purely (or perhaps, more accurately, principally) national, this itself presents difficulties, though not fundamentally different to those presented by traditional international trade.[365] However, the number of international contracts being made has greatly increased over time, and the proportion of these business-to-customer has increased at an even greater rate.[366] This has brought with it difficulties for national regulators and enforcement agencies, to whom their nationals turn when presented with a consumer grievance. The response from the regulators is varied, but that from the courts has been to apply national consumer laws over Internet contracts, wherever possible.[367] This presents important conflict of laws questions. For how may a consumer obtain legal redress against an Internet-based trader except by complex litigation through national courts? Consumer laws by their nature should be consumer-friendly, and should enable consumers to have recourse through national courts. Indeed, conflict of laws principles do allow laws to be applied extraterritorially.

Historically, there has been a legislative presumption against the extra-territorial application of public law statutes, as a matter of statutory interpretation.[368] This is based on a historical concern not to infringe on the sovereignty of other states (or provinces) by purporting to regulate conduct that occurs wholly within the boundaries of another jurisdiction.[369]

---

28 November 2003).

[365]See Richard M. Bird, *Taxation and e-commerce*, 38 THE CANADIAN BUSINESS L. J. 466 (2003).

[366]See Udaykiran Vallamsetty, Krishna Kant & Prasant Mohapatra, *Characterisation of E-Commerce Traffic*, 3 ELECTRONIC COMMERCE RESEARCH 167 (2003).

[367]This is also effected by the relevant national laws and international conventions — see, for example, Peter Stone, *Internet consumer contracts and European private international law*, 9 INFORM. & COMMS. TECHN. L. 5-15 (2000).

[368]Though there are important exceptions, including in the consumer law field. For example, the Fair Trading Act 1986 (NZ) states, in s 3, that "This Act extends to the engaging in conduct outside New Zealand by any person resident or carrying on business in New Zealand to the extent that such conduct relates to the supply of goods or services, or the granting of interests in land, within New Zealand."

[369]See Roger Tassé & Maxime Faille, *Online Consumer Protection in Canada: The Problem of Regulatory Jurisdiction*, 2 INTERNET & E-COMMERCE L. IN

Customary international law however permits a nation to apply its law to extraterritorial behaviour with substantial local effect,[370] as well as the extraterritorial conduct of its citizens or domiciliary.[371]

The U.S. Federal Trade Commission (FTC) acts against fraudulent and deceptive foreign e-businesses that harm U.S. consumers.[372] The FTC Act gives the FTC authority over acts "in or affecting commerce" and defines "commerce" to include "commerce with foreign nations."[373] The act also gives the FTC specific authority to investigate practices that "may affect the foreign trade of the United States."[374]

US anti-trust laws provide a broad base for assertion of jurisdiction, which permit jurisdiction over foreign activities that have "a direct, substantial, and reasonably foreseeable effect" on commerce in the US.[375] However, extraterritorial enforcement by the U.S. often generates a perception abroad of a sort of "United States imperialism."[376] This is particularly so where the effects are profound.[377] The extraterritorial

---

CANADA 41 (2000-01). See also *Buchanan v. Rucker*, 9 East 192; 103 ER 546, 547 (1808): "Can the Island of Tobago pass a law to bind the rights of the whole world?"

[370]*The Case of the 'S.S. Lotus'*, P.C.I.J. (ser A) No 10, 18-251927.

[371]*Blackmer v. U.S.*, 284 U.S. 421, 436 (1932) ; *U.S. v. Rech*, 780 F. 2d 1541, 1543 n 2 (11th cir, 1986).

[372]See Roscoe B. Starek III & Lynda M. Rozell, *The Federal Trade Commission's commitment to on-line consumer protection*, 15 THE JOHN MARSHALL J. OF COMPUTER & INFORM. L. 679-702 (1997).

[373]Federal Trade Commission Act, 15 U.S.C. § 41-44, ss 5, 6.

[374]See Jodie Bernstein, Director, Bureau of Consumer Protection, US Federal Trade Commission, Fighting Internet Fraud: A Global Effort, 5 ECONOMIC PERSPECTIVES, AN ELECTRONIC J. OF THE U.S. DEPARTMENT OF STATE (2000), available at <http://usinfo.state.gov/J.s/ites/0500/ijee/ftc2.htm> (as at 1 December 2003).

[375]From the Sherman Anti-trust Act (1890) Title 15 U.S.C. §§ 1-7; Federal Trade Commission Act (1914) Title 15 U.S.C. §§ 41-51.

[376]See Robert Pitofsky, *Competition Policy in a Global Economy – Today And Tomorrow*, The European Institute's Eighth Annual Transatlantic Seminar on Trade and Investment Washington, D.C., USA, 4 November 1998, available at <http://www.techlawJ..com/atr/81104ftc.htm> (as at 1 December 2003).

[377]As, for example, in *Hartford Fire Insurance Co v. California*, 509 U.S. 764 (1993) [where U.K. reinsurers were compelled to adhere to the U.S. regulatory regime].

application of the U.S. antitrust laws caused considerable disquiet in other countries:

Where a transnational antitrust issue is really a manifestation of a policy conflict between governments, it should be recognised that there may be no applicable international law to resolve the conflict. In such cases, resolution should be sought through the normal methods of consultation and negotiation. For one government to seek to resolve the conflict in its favour by invoking its national law before its domestic tribunals is not the rule of law but an application, in judicial guise, of the principle that economic might is right.[378]

Other countries have also applied their laws extraterritorially.[379] But the larger the economy the greater the influence, and perhaps, the greater the resentment of smaller economies. In *Libman*,[380] the Supreme Court of Canada ruled that "it is sufficient that there be a 'real and substantial link'" between the proscribed conduct and the jurisdiction seeking to apply and enforce its law.[381] Clearly, the "real and substantial link" test for the proper assertion of prescriptive jurisdiction will often result in more than one, and perhaps many, jurisdictions being capable of properly asserting authority over conduct that has effects in more than one jurisdiction. It is this fact that suggests the need for clearer prescriptive jurisdictional rules,[382] especially for consumer laws. This is a constitutional dilemma, one which strikes at the heart of the nation-state.

Appropriately, when we are considering developments of supra-national laws, it is the European Union, the first successful supra-national state in modern times,[383] which has led the way. The European Union has been active in developing rules relating to jurisdictional issues in the context of e-commerce.[384] Undoubtedly this is facilitated by the existence of a

---

[378]See J.S. Stanford, *The Application of the Sherman Act to Conduct Outside the United States: A View from Abroad*, 11 CORNELL INTERN. L. J. 195 *(1978)*. *See also* Joseph P. Griffin, *Foreign Governmental Reactions to U.S. Assertion of Extraterritorial Jurisdiction*, 6 George Mason L. Rev. 505 (1998).

[379]As for example, the High Court of Australia found *in Dow Jones & Company Inc v. Gutnick*, 194 ALR 433 (2002).

[380]*R v. Libman*, 2 S.C.R. 178 (1985).

[381]*R v. Libman*, 2 S.C.R. 178 (1985).

[382]See Roger Tassé & Maxime Faille, *Online Consumer Protection in Canada: The Problem of Regulatory Jurisdiction*, 2 INTERNET & E-COMMERCE L. IN CANADA 41 (2000-01).

[383]Though it may be questioned whether it is premature to categorise it as successful. Earlier empires, such as Rome, may also be regarded as successful supranational states.

[384]For instance, see Peter Stone, *Internet consumer contracts and European private*

treaty-based regime integral to the development of the Single Market, a regime that, perforce, has long provided for resolution of jurisdictional matters.[385] The primary instruments in the civil or private law context in this regard have been the Brussels Convention on Jurisdiction and the Enforcement of Judgments in Civil and Commercial Matters, which deal with jurisdiction to adjudicate matters as well as with the enforcement of extra-territorial judgments, and the Rome Convention on the Law Applicable to Contractual Obligations.[386] The latter determines which state's substantive law shall be applied in cross-border disputes.[387] The Brussels 2 Regulation is now also applicable.[388] But none of these have direct application to consumer laws.

Most private international law rules and principles are evolving, and may be traced some distance into the past. There is nothing new about courts being called upon to decide which court will have jurisdiction, which law will apply, or how judgment will be enforced. But these questions are rendered more difficult by the virtual nature of the Internet. Complex litigation – or arbitration – may be possible in business-to-business transactions involving millions of dollars, but are impracticable for business-to-consumer transactions and smaller commercial contracts. If governments fail to resolve this they fail in their prime function – and risk obsolescence.

Legal systems have developed rules for regulating disputes. But nineteenth and twentieth century conflict of laws principles do not satisfy the requirements of consumer laws. These require immediate, simple, low-cost remedies.

For the most part the Internet is international, and its users are not adequately served by existing laws with respect to conflict of laws.[389] The

---

international law, 9 INFORM. & COMMS. TECHN. L. 5-15 (2000).

[385]See K.P.E. LASOK, THE EUROPEAN COURT OF JUSTICE: PRACTICE AND PROCEDURE (2d ed. 1994).

[386]Convention on the law applicable to contractual obligations, Rome, 19 June 1980.

[387]Convention on Jurisdiction and the Enforcement of Judgments in Civil and Commercial matters, Brussels, 27 September 1968; Convention on the law applicable to contractual obligations, Rome, 19 June 1980.

[388]The Council of the European Union regulation (EC) N° 1348/2000 of 29 May 2000 on the service in the Member States of judicial and extrajudicial documents in civil or commercial matters. This came into force March 2002.

[389]Though not necessarily because of any profound difference between cyberspace and territorial space, but rather because of the complexity of cyberspace; See Jack L. Goldsmith, *Against Cyberanarchy*, 65 U. CHICAGO L.

efficacy of the concept of "closest and most real connection"[390] is also reduced, in that no part of the world is any more directly affected than any other by events on the web, as information is available simultaneously to anyone with a connection to the Internet.[391] In the field of protection of intellectual property rights the same is also probably true.[392]

The difficulty facing national jurisdictions is partly one of enforcement,[393] which has led to other forms of regulation, including (but not limited to) trans-national, international, institutional, sectoral and private.[394] There are an increasing number of examples of private control or self-regulatory control, sometimes involving codes.[395] Unfortunately these disparate approaches exasperate the already marked divisions.[396] Nor are there signs that international co-operation will be practical outside narrow legal fields such as copyright and operations against cyber-crime.[397]

To date, most efforts to address this deficiency have concentrated on

---

REV. 1199-1250 (1998).

[390]*McConnell Dowell Constructors Ltd v. Lloyd's Syndicate 396*, 2 N.Z.L.R. 257 (1988) (CA); LAWRENCE COLLINS (ed), DICEY AND MORRIS ON THE CONFLICT OF LAWS ch 32 (13th ed. 2000).

[391]See David R. Johnson & David G. Post, *Law and Borders: The Rise of Law in Cyberspace*, 48 STANFORD L. REV. 1367 (1996). It can of course be argued that a webpage can be 'directed' at certain countries.

[392]See Dan L. Burk, *Muddy Rules for Cyberspace*, 21 CARDOZO L. REV. 121 (1998-99), available at <http://www.cardozo.yu.edu/cardlrev/v21n1/burk.pdf> (as at 1 December 2003).

[393]It also has constitutional implications if states relinquish enforcement to other bodies or countries.

[394]See, for example, LAWRENCE LESSIG, CODE AND OTHER LAWS OF CYBERSPACE (1999); CHRISTOPHER MARSDEN, REGULATING THE GLOBAL INFORMATION SOCIETY (2000).

[395]See Joseph A. Cannataci & Jeanne Pia Mifsud Bonnici, *Can self-regulation satisfy the transnational requisite of successful Internet regulation?*, 17 INTERN. REV. OF L., Computers & Techn. 51-61 (2003); Philip J. Weiser, *Internet governance, standard setting, and self-regulation*, 28 NORTHERN KENTUCKY L. REV. 822-846 (2001).

[396]Such as between the U.S. and the European Union.

[397]The WIPO, Council of Europe convention, respectively; World Intellectual Property Organisation Copyright Treaty, adopted in Geneva on 20 December, 1996; Convention on Cybercrime, Budapest, 23 November 2001 (ETS No 185). See also Jonathan B. Wolf, *War games meets the internet: Chasing 21st century cybercriminals with old laws and little money*, 28 AM. J. OF CRIMINAL L. 95 (2000).

increased international co-operation. Some of this is web-based, such as the econsumer.gov website, which tracks consumer complaints from a number of countries.[398] This co-operation often results in de facto self-regulation of the Internet. The Organisation for Economic Co-operation and Development has issued guidelines which calling on the organisation's 30 member states – which include the US, Japan, Germany and the U.K. – to cooperate in the fight against international fraud.[399] This clearly allude to the problem of unsolicited commercial e-mail. The Internet may not be outside the law, but the application and enforcement of laws remain difficult. Ultimately, a new legal regime may emerge, one which responds to the difficultly of regulating a technology which has either insufficient, or too many, laws.[400]

Whether the Internet can, or should, become subject to international law is a question the answer to which could be as seminal as the adoption of the Law of Oléron[401] or the resolution of the Thirty Years War at the Treaty of Westphalia – the so-called Diet of Worms.[402] Perhaps the response of governments to the age of electronic communications cannot be limited to the piecemeal adoption of laws in response to individual problems.

The Internet and the advent of almost instantaneous communications have had and will continue to have major effects upon international trade law. In particular, evidential rules founded on former paper-based procedures have not proven to be flexible enough to accommodate the advent of the Internet and contracts made in cyberspace.[403] Just as the law

---

[398] <http://www.econsumer.gov/> (as at 1 December 2003). As yet, such tools are only partly successful, due to incomplete coverage and limited knowledge of their existence among consumers.

[399] ORGANISATION FOR ECONOMIC CO-OPERATION AND DEVELOPMENT, OECD GUIDELINES FOR PROTECTING CONSUMERS FROM FRAUDULENT AND DECEPTIVE COMMERCIAL PRACTICES ACROSS BORDERS, 11 June 2003 (2003).

[400] Too many, if this is seen as primarily a jurisdictional problem in traditional conflict of laws terms.

[401] According to tradition, these were adopted in Castile by Alphonso X in the 13th century, derived from the code founded in the republic of Rhodes and adopted by the Romans and other maritime powers of the Mediterranean, and were introduced into England by Richard I. Originally they were connected with wine shipments from France, but afterwards took on a wider significance; SIR WILLIAM BLACKSTONE, COMMENTARIES ON THE LAW OF ENGLAND, Bk 1 ch 13 (1983).

[402] 1648. See BENNO TESCHKE, THE MYTH OF 1648: CLASS, GEOPOLITICS, AND THE MAKING OF MODERN INTERNATIONAL RELATIONS (2003).

merchant evolved to accommodate contracts negotiated between parties who were physically apart, so cyberspace law must do so for the electronic age.

Traditionally, the formation of legal norms for conducting trade was by states, subject to certain principles accepted by the international community. But this has proven inadequate for the control of electronic commerce, because this can be said to be truly international, having no physical presence. The new environment has necessitated an increased degree of international co-ordination, if not co-operation. Unlike the evolutionary development of the *lex mercatoria*, the advent of electronic communications has resulted in the enforced adoption of international norms, such as the UNCITRAL Model Law on Electronic Commerce.[404]

This poses a threat to state sovereignty. It is no longer possible for the nation-state to be the sole, or even prime, regulator of economic norms. Decisions respecting the forms of law will be made not at the national level, but internationally. These will be made by political blocks such as the European Union and the United Nations, and, in some instances, by non-governmental organisations. The result could be the evolution of an international cyberspace law. But there are wider implications for national legal systems which cannot be ignored. Failure to protect and encourage international trade could well result in states being bypassed economically in favour of those which are more active.

(b) (ii) The Internet and the state

A prediction made some years ago that the Internet would change international law because it would erode the dominance of the traditional sovereign state[405] has not become reality yet.[406] But it is potentially a threat

---

[403]See Gregory P. Joseph, *Internet and email evidence*, 19 THE COMPUTER & INTERNET LAWYER 17-22 (2002).

[404]In the U.S., the Digital Millennium Copyright Act (1998), Pub. L. No. 105-304, 112 Stat. 2860, 2905, in New Zealand the Electronic Transactions Act 2000 (NZ).

[405]See Henry H. Perritt, *The Internet is Changing International Law*, 73 CHICAGO-KENT L. REV. 997 (1998).

[406]Franz C. Mayer, *The Internet and Public International Law – Worlds Apart?*, (2001) 12 EUROPEAN J. OF INTERN. L. 617, 621. It might perhaps be helpful to remember the short story "Dial F for Frankenstein", by the distinguished writer Sir Arthur C. Clarke. This concerned the formation of a worldwide telephone network (in many ways equivalent to the Internet). Unfortunately for humankind, the network becomes self-aware, and

to state sovereignty,[407] and therefore has profound constitutional implications.

Partly because of the international – and unregulated (or self-regulating) nature of the Internet, there has been a tendency to claim that the changes we observe in notions of sovereignty, the state, jurisdiction, and law in general are caused by the Internet.[408] It has been said that the very nature and growing importance of the net calls for a fundamental re-examination of the institutional structure within which rule-making takes place.[409] But, as has been observed by various writers, globalisation of commerce is not a new phenomenon.[410] Nor would it necessarily be valid to

---

decidedly malignant; published in THE WIND FROM THE SUN: STORIES OF THE SPACE AGE (1962).

[407]See Georgios Zekos, *Internet or Electronic Technology: A Threat to State Sovereignty*, 3 J. OF INFORM., L. & TECHN. (1999), available at <http://elj.warwick.ac.UK/jilt/99-3/zekos.html> (as at 28 November 2003); David G. Post & David R. Johnson, *'Chaos Prevailing on Every Continent': Towards a New Theory of Decentralised Decision-Making in Complex Systems*, 14 June 1999, Social Science Research Network Electronic Library, available   at <http://papers.ssrn.com/sol3/delivery.cfm/99032613.pdf?abstractid=157 692> (as at 1 December 2003). See also Dan L. Burk, *Federalism in Cyberspace*, 28 CONNECTICUT L. REV. 1095 (1996); Joel R. Reidenberg, *Governing Networks and Rule-Making in Cyberspace*, in BRIAN KAHIN & CHARLES NESSON (eds), BORDERS IN CYBERSPACE, 84, 85-87 (1997).

[408]It has been said that the very nature and growing importance of the Internet requires a fundamental re-examination of the institutional structure within which rulemaking takes place: see David R. Johnson & David G. Post, *And How Shall the Net be_Governed? A Meditation on the Relative Virtues of Decentralised, Emergent Law*, draft paper at Cyberspace Law Institute Papers on Cyberspace Law, available at <http://www.cli.org/emdraft.html> (as at 28 November 2003); Anne Wells Branscomb, *Jurisdictional Quandaries for Global Networks*, in LINDA M. HARASIM (ed), GLOBAL NETWORKS: COMPUTERS AND INTERNATIONAL COMMUNICATION (1993).

[409]See David G. Post & David R. Johnson, *'Chaos Prevailing on Every Continent': Towards a New Theory of Decentralised Decision-Making in Complex Systems*, Social Science   Research   Network   Electronic   Library <http://papers.ssrn.com/sol3/delivery.cfm/99032613.pdf?abstractid=157 692> (as at 1 December 2003).

[410]The analogy between the rise of a separate law of cyberspace and the Law Merchant has been observed: see I. Trotter Hardy, *The Proper Legal Regime for 'Cyberspace'*, 55 U. PITTSBURGH L. REV. 993, 1020 (1994); Noel Cox, *The Regulation of Cyberspace and the Loss of National Sovereignty*, 11 INFORM. &

assign to the one cause a range of paradigm changes in society, economics and governance.[411] Our existing international law is predicated on the existence of the sovereign state. The notions of sovereignty and statehood were once among the most important aspects of public international law. We may ask whether the Internet, as one of the newest and most potent technological innovations, threatens this dominance.

As Hall has noted, primarily international law governs the relations of independent states, but "to a limited extent ... it may also govern the relations of certain communities of analogous character."[412] Nor is he alone, similar views being expressed by other writers.[413] Lawrence also wrote that the subjects of international law are sovereign states, "and those other political bodies which, though lacking many of the attributes of sovereign states, possess some to such an extent as to make them real, but imperfect, international persons."[414] Whereas these scholars tended to define subjects of international law as states and certain unusual exceptions, there are others who go further in opening up the realm of reasonable subjects of the law of nations.[415]

The advent of the sovereign cyberspace is as far away as it ever was, but it remains true however that our existing international laws are predicated on the existence of the sovereign state. Its heyday was perhaps in the late nineteenth century, when sovereign states enjoyed almost unfettered independence of action.[416] These were subject only to the regulation of their diplomatic and military action, principally by the Law of Armed Conflict, or the Laws of War.[417] International law has been called "the sum of the rules or usages which civilised states have agreed shall be binding upon them in their dealings with one another."[418] But the norms of

---

COMMUN. TECHN. L. 241 (2002).

[411]As was seen in the Middle Ages, for example.

[412]See WILLIAM E. HALL, A TREATISE ON INTERNATIONAL LAW ed A. Pearce Higgins (8th ed. 1924).

[413]See GEORGE SCHWARZENBERGER, A MANUAL OF INTERNATIONAL LAW (1947); WOLFGANG FRIEDMANN, THE CHANGING STRUCTURE OF INTERNATIONAL LAW (1964).

[414]T.J. LAWRENCE, THE PRINCIPLES OF INTERNATIONAL LAW (1924).

[415]See E. Lauterpacht, *The Subjects of the Law of Nations*, 63 L.Q.R. 444 (1947).

[416]See W. ROSS JOHNSTON, SOVEREIGNTY AND PROTECTION: A STUDY OF BRITISH JURISDICTIONAL IMPERIALISM IN THE LATE NINETEENTH CENTURY (1973).

[417]See JACK GRUNAWALT & MICHAEL N. SCHMITT (eds), THE LAW OF MILITARY OPERATIONS: LIBER AMICORUM (1998).

[418]*West Rand Central Gold Mining Co v. The King*, 2 K.B. 391 (1905) quoting Lord Russell of Killowen in his address at Saratoga in 1876. See also SIR

international law, even in the nineteenth century, which saw the acme of the concept of the sovereign nation-state, recognised multiple sources of authority.[419] Many modern philosophers of law (not to mention political scientists) have concluded that using largely nineteenth century concepts of sovereignty as a benchmark of what political authority should be is either teleological at best or wrong at worst.[420] We are now questioning the place of the sovereign state, not because we necessarily wish to abolish it, but because we must question their place. The Internet and globalisation have raised questions about the place of the state, when it is possible to communicate in real time with people across the globe, without regard to place of residence, and to conduct business with them.[421]

The traditional juristic theory of territorial sovereignty, with the King being supreme ruler within the confines of his kingdom, originated as two distinct concepts. The King acknowledged no superior in temporal matters, and within his kingdom the King was emperor.[422] If the Holy Roman Emperor had legal supremacy within the *terrae imperii*, the confines of the empire, theories of the sovereignty of kings were not needed, for they had merely de facto power.[423] In Roman law it was originally considered that the

---

MICHAEL HOWARD, GEORGE J. ANDREOPOULOS & MARK R. SHULMAN (eds), THE LAWS OF WAR – CONSTRAINTS ON WARFARE IN THE WESTERN WORLD (1994); J. GILLINGHAM & J.C. HOLT (eds), WAR AND GOVERNMENT IN THE MIDDLE AGES (1984).

[419]See MAURICE H. KEEN, THE LAWS OF WAR IN THE LATE MIDDLE AGES (1965). International law has been called "the sum of the rules or usages which civilised states have agreed shall be binding upon them in their dealings with one another"; *West Rand Central Gold Mining Co v. The King*, 2 K.B. 391 (1905). Standard histories of the laws of war include ADAM ROBERTS & RICHARD GUELLF (eds), LAWS OF WAR (2000); GEOFFREY BEST, HUMANITY IN WARFARE: THE MODERN HISTORY OF THE INTERNATIONAL LAW OF ARMED CONFLICT (1980).

[420]KENNETH PENNINGTON, THE PRINCE AND THE LAW, 1200-1600: SOVEREIGNTY AND RIGHTS IN THE WESTERN LEGAL TRADITION, 121(1993).

[421]It also encourages the use of the English language, though there are signs that this dominance of English may be declining. See *Global Internet Statistics*, Global Reach, available at <http://www.glreach.com/globstats/> (as at 10 December 2003) [35% of users in 2003 spoke English as their native language, and 65% were non-English – of which the largest group was the 12% who spoke Chinese].

[422]See Walter Ullmann, *This Realm of England is an Empire*, 30 J. OF ECCLESIASTICAL HISTORY 175 (1979).

[423]A similar argument was made for the Pope's legal supremacy; See

emperor's power had been bestowed upon him by the people,[424] but when Rome became a Christian state his power was regarded as coming from God.[425] In the U.S. God also had been recognised as the source of governmental authority, although it is commonly thought in a republican or democratic government "all power is inherent in the people."[426]

Sovereignty remained essentially de jure authority.[427] Emperor Frederick I Barbarossa saw the advantages of Roman law and legal science for his ambitions and his inception of absolutism.[428] This led to the growth of royal absolutism, and eventually to the emergence of opposition to this, throughout Europe.[429] This was not merely power without legitimacy.[430] Mediæval jurists cared not whether the emperor had jurisdiction and authority over kings and princes, but focused on his power to usurp the rights of his subjects. Whether this power was de facto or de jure was unimportant.[431]

HYGINUS EUGENE CARDINALE, THE HOLY SEE AND THE INTERNATIONAL ORDER (1976); WALTER ULLMANN, THE GROWTH OF PAPAL GOVERNMENT IN THE MIDDLE AGES: A STUDY IN THE IDEOLOGICAL RELATION OF CLERICAL TO LAY POWER (2d ed. 1965).

[424]"S.P.Q.R." ("Senatus Populusque Romae") – for the Senate and People of Rome, was a was a kind of "motto" of the Roman Republic, but which never passed entirely out of use until the later years of the empire.

[425]See DAVID POTTER, PROPHETS AND EMPERORS: HUMAN AND DIVINE AUTHORITY FROM AUGUSTUS TO THEODOSIUS (1994).

[426]This is reflected in the words of the pledge of allegiance to the flag of the U.S. – "one nation under God" – adopted 1954 when President Dwight D. Eisenhower approved adding the words "under God" to the existing pledge, despite the constitutional separation of church and state in the U.S. (in the First Amendment of the U.S. Constitution: "Congress shall make no law respecting an establishment of religion, or prohibiting the free exercise thereof.").

[427]J.P. Canning, Law, sovereignty and corporation theory, 1300-1450, in J.H. BURNS (ed), THE CAMBRIDGE HISTORY OF MEDIÆVAL POLITICAL THOUGHT C.350-C.1450, 465-467 (1988).

[428]HAROLD J. BERMAN, LAW AND REVOLUTION: THE FORMATION OF THE WESTERN LEGAL TRADITION, ch 14 (1983).

[429]KENNETH PENNINGTON, THE PRINCE AND THE LAW, 1200-1600: SOVEREIGNTY AND RIGHTS IN THE WESTERN LEGAL TRADITION, 12 (1993).

[430]J.P. Canning, Law, sovereignty and corporation theory, 1300-1450, in J.H. BURNS (ed), THE CAMBRIDGE HISTORY OF MEDIÆVAL POLITICAL THOUGHT C.350-C.1450, 467-471 (1988).

[431]KENNETH PENNINGTON, THE PRINCE AND THE LAW, 1200-1600:

But in the course of the nineteenth century the notion of state sovereignty prevailed,[432] and after World War One, the nation-state.[433] This was reinforced by de-colonisation after World War Two.[434] A counter-movement is now underway. The Internet, as a transnational system of communications, has shown signs of developing a distinct legal form.[435] But the Law Merchant evolved, as did other forms of international customary law, through usage and practice. It did not require a central authority, and nor was it inconsistent with sovereignty, de facto or de jure – and it developed over a considerable period of time.[436]

Even if a sovereign cyberspace is unlikely to develop as some have predicted, it may be that there is scope for the creation of novel forms of new states,[437] but such scope appears to be restricted. Statehood has

---

SOVEREIGNTY AND RIGHTS IN THE WESTERN LEGAL TRADITION, 30 (1993).

[432]See W. ROSS JOHNSTON, SOVEREIGNTY AND PROTECTION: A STUDY OF BRITISH JURISDICTIONAL IMPERIALISM IN THE LATE NINETEENTH CENTURY (1973).

[433]See MONTSERRAT GUIBERNAU, NATIONALISMS: THE NATION-STATE AND NATIONALISM IN THE TWENTIETH CENTURY (1996).

[434]See ROBERT CARR, BLACK NATIONALISM IN THE NEW WORLD: READING THE AFRICAN AMERICAN AND WEST INDIAN EXPERIENCE (2002).

[435]Though a separate jurisdiction for cyberspace has been rejected by the courts; *New Zealand Post v. Leng*, 3 N.Z.L.R. 219, 226 (1993) per Williams J.

[436]See Robert D. Cooter, *Structural adjudication and the new law merchant: A model of decentralised law*, 12 INTERN. REV. OF L. & ECONOMICS 215 (1994).

[437]For the recognition of new states see C. Hillgruber, *The Admission of New States to the International Community*, 9 EUROPEAN J. OF INTERN. LAw 491 (1998), available at <http://www.ejil.org/J./Vol9/No3/ab3.html> (as at 28 November 2003); T. GRANT, THE RECOGNITION OF STATES: LAW AND PRACTICE IN DEBATE AND EVOLUTION (1999). The European practice of recognising new States in Eastern Europe and in the former Soviet Union in 1991-1992 was based on the guidelines adopted by the European Commission Member States on 16 December 1991 (see 31 INTERN. LEGAL MATERIALS 1486 (1992)). The list of criteria lays down the conditions that had to be fulfilled before the Community was prepared to recognise the new States, and thus to agree to their admission to the community of States and to the international community. It has been claimed that the conditions listed in the guidelines are merely the criteria for the establishment of diplomatic relations – something which is in the political discretion of the States in any case – and not requirements for statehood in the sense of international law; M. Weller, *The International Response to the Dissolution of the*

hitherto been the necessary precondition of tax haven status. For only a state is able to impose – and repeal – taxation and regulatory laws.[438]

Traditionally only a state was regarded as an international person, capable of having rights and duties under international law.[439] That entities other than states might be the subjects of international law is even today not a universally accepted idea,[440] and exactly which entities do have this status is an even more controversial topic. Early in the twentieth century, Hall noted that international law primarily governs the relations of independent states, but "to a limited extent ... it may also govern the relations of certain communities of analogous character."[441] At about the

---

Socialist Federal Republic of Yugoslavia, 86 AM. J. OF INTERN. LAW 569, 588, 604 (1992). See also S. Talmon, *Recognition of Governments: An Analysis of the New British Policy and Practice*, 58 BRITISH YEARBOOK OF INTERN. LAW 231, 250-251 (1992); Montevideo Convention on the Rights and Duties of States, 26 December 1933, 49 Stat. 3097; U.S.A. Treaty Series 881, entered into force 26 December 1934, in MANLEY OTTMER HUDSON (ed), INTERNATIONAL LEGISLATION (1931-50) Vol 6, p 620; IAN BROWNLIE, PRINCIPLES OF PUBLIC INTERNATIONAL LAW, ch 5 (5th ed. 1998). Although the application of the Convention is confined to Latin America, it is regarded as declaratory of customary international law. See also *Island of Palmas Arbitration Case*, No. xix (2) Reports of Intern. Arbitral Awards 829 (1928); 22 AM. J. OF INTERN. LAW 986 (1928); 4 ARBITRATION DECISIONS 3.

[438]See Noel Cox, *Tax and regulatory avoidance through non-traditional alternatives to tax havens*, 9 NEW ZEALAND BUSINESS L. Q. 10-32 (2003).

[439]The assumptions of international lawyers about the near-exclusive role of States seem to be largely shared by international relations theory. See K. Abbott, *Modern International Relations Theory: A Prospectus for International Lawyers*, 14 YALE J. OF INTERN. LAW 335 (1989).

[440]See S. Charnovitz, *Opening the WTO to Non-Governmental Interests*, 24 FORDHAM INTERN. L. J. 173 (2000); LEGAL AFFAIRS COMMITTEE OF THE PARLIAMENTARY ASSEMBLY OF THE COUNCIL OF EUROPE, LEGAL STATUS OF INTERNATIONAL NON-GOVERNMENTAL ORGANISATIONS IN EUROPE, ed D. Smith (1986); International Law Commission, *Status, privileges and immunities of international organisations, their officials, experts, etc*, in ANALYTICAL GUIDE TO THE PRACTICE OF THE INTERNATIONAL LAW COMMISSION, available at <http://www.un.org/law/ilc/guide/gfra.htm> (as at 1 December 2003). See also European Convention on the Recognition of the Legal Personality of International Non-Governmental Organisations, 24 April 1986, E.T.S. 124, entered into force 1 January 1991.

[441]See WILLIAM E. HALL, A TREATISE ON INTERNATIONAL LAW ed A. Pearce Higgins (8th ed. 1924). Nor was he alone, similar views being

same time, Lawrence wrote that the subjects of international law were sovereign states, "and those other political bodies which, though lacking many of the attributes of sovereign states, possess some to such an extent as to make them real, but imperfect, international persons."[442] Whereas these scholars tended to define subjects of international law as states and certain unusual exceptions, there are others who went further in opening up the realm of reasonable subjects of the law of nations. Notable among them was Lauterpacht. In his view:[443]

International practice shows that persons and bodies other than states are often made subjects of international rights and duties, that such developments are not inconsistent with the structure of international law and that in each particular case the question whether a person or a body is a subject of international law must be answered in a pragmatic manner by reference to actual experience and to the reason of the law as distinguished from the preconceived notion as to who can be the subjects of international law.

Indeed, it has since been observed that "a look at history, however, tells us that conceptions of world order have by no means always been shaped by the model of sovereign co-equal actors with a territorial basis."[444] The recognition of non-state entities has indeed become more pronounced since the 1960s.[445]

The status of organisations in international law is less controversial

---

expressed by other writers: GEORGE SCHWARZENBERGER, A MANUAL OF INTERNATIONAL LAW, 48 (1947); WOLFGANG FRIEDMANN, THE CHANGING STRUCTURE OF INTERNATIONAL LAW, 213-215 (1964).

[442]T.J. LAWRENCE, THE PRINCIPLES OF INTERNATIONAL LAW, 69 (7d ed. 1925).

[443]See E. Lauterpacht, *The Subjects of the Law of Nations*, 63 L.Q.REV. 444 (1947). See also C. Schreuer, *The Waning of the Sovereign State: Towards A New Paradigm for International Law?*, 4 EUROPEAN J. OF INTERN. LAW 447 (1993), available at <http://www.ejil.org/J./Vol4/No4/art1.html> (as at 1 December 2003).

[444]See C. Schreuer, *The Waning of the Sovereign State: Towards A New Paradigm for International Law?*, 4 EUROPEAN J. OF INTERN. LAW 447 (1993), available at <http://www.ejil.org/J./Vol4/No4/art1.html> (as at 1 December 2003).

[445]See C. Schreuer, *The Waning of the Sovereign State: Towards A New Paradigm for International Law?*, 4 EUROPEAN J. OF INTERN. LAW 447 (1993), available at <http://www.ejil.org/J./Vol4/No4/art1.html> (as at 1 December 2003); M. Koskenniemi, *The Future of Statehood*, 32 HARV. INTERN. L. J. 397 (1991); N. MacCormick, *Beyond the Sovereign States*, 56 MODERN L. REV. 1 (1993).

than the assumption of rights and duties by individuals or groups of individuals. In 1949, the International Court of Justice recognised the United Nations Organisation as an international person,[446] marking an important stage in the process whereby an ever-increasing number of modern international organisations are recognised as having personality in international law. That is not, however, the same thing as saying that such an organisation is a state, or that its legal personality and rights and duties are the same as those of a state.[447]

While it is possible for organisations and individuals to be subjects of international law, states remain the dominant agents in world politics and the dominant actors in international law. This dominance has led some theorists to distinguish "subjects" of the law from "objects" of the law, suggesting that although entities other than states may have rights and duties in international law, these rights are conferred upon them by states and, presumably, may be taken away by states.[448] It is possibly more correct now to regard international law as a body of rules that binds states and other agents in world politics in their relations with one another, and that is considered to have the status of law.[449]

There are now many organisations operating on an international plane. Whilst many such organisations, such as the European Union and the United Nations Organisation, receive ambassadors from member countries, the Sovereign Military Order of Malta almost alone among international organisations claims the right to send representatives to other states for the purpose of carrying on diplomatic negotiations,[450] as well as to receive

---

[446]*Reparation for Injuries Suffered in the Service of the UN*, 4 I.C.J.R. 179 (1949).

[447]"[The UN] is a subject of international law and capable of possessing international rights and duties, and ... it has capacity to maintain its rights by bringing international claims"; see *Reparation for Injuries Suffered in the Service of the UN*, 4 I.C.J.R. 179, pp 178, 179 (1949).

[448]GEORGE SCHWARZENBERGER AND E.D. BROWN, A MANUAL OF INTERNATIONAL LAW, 42 (6th ed. 1976).

[449]H. BULL, THE ANARCHICAL SOCIETY: A STUDY OF ORDER IN WORLD POLITICS, 127 (1977); E. Lauterpacht, *The Subjects of the Law of Nations*, 63 L.Q.REV. 444 (1947); ROSALYN HIGGINS, THE DEVELOPMENT OF INTERNATIONAL LAW THROUGH THE POLITICAL ORGANS OF THE UN, 1 (1963); P. JESSUP, A MODERN LAW OF NATIONS (1968); J.G. CASTEL, INTERNATIONAL LAW: CHIEFLY AS INTERPRETED AND APPLIED IN CANADA, 1 (3d ed. 1976).

[450]The Holy See is in a similar position, though the existence of the Vatican City complicates the situation. It is important to realise that it is the Holy See which is recognised by the United Nations, and not Vatican City State (which fulfils the fuller requirements for State sovereignty). In United

representatives from other states for the same purpose.[451] Most importantly, the Sovereign Military Order of Malta claims, and is sometimes acknowledged by states, to be a sovereign state in its own right.[452] This status has been claimed since at least the fourteenth century, well before international law began to accord legal personality to international organisations.[453] But the Order is not unique in such claims. Its own parent body, the Holy See, has for long been regarded as sovereign, apparently even when the papacy was without territorial possessions.[454] Territorial possessions gave both the Holy See and the Sovereign Military Order of Malta their status as sovereign states, but the loss of territory did not necessarily extinguish that status.[455]

Nations documents, the term "Holy See" is used except in texts concerning the International Telecommunications Union and the Universal Postal Union, where the term "Vatican City State" is used. States do not entertain diplomatic relations with Vatican City State, but with the Holy See. The term "Holy See" refers to the supreme authority of the Church, the Pope as Bishop of Rome and head of the College of Cardinals. It is the central government of the Roman Catholic Church: See Archbishop R. Martino, *A Short History of the Holy See's Diplomacy*, available at <http://www.holyseemission.org/short_history.html> (as at 1 December 2003).

[451]The Order was also involved in the Geneva Conventions, and is a member of the International Red Cross. The European Communities also accredit some ambassadors. Both the Order of Malta and the International Red Cross have had permanent observer status at the United Nations since 1994. For a list of permanent members, non-member States with permanent observer missions at UN headquarters, and entities with a standing invitation to participate as observers in the sessions and work of the General Assembly and maintaining permanent offices at headquarters, see <http://www.un.org/Overview/missions.htm#nperm> (as at 1 December 2003).

[452]For example, San Marino acknowledged the Order as a sovereign State in a treaty of amity in 1935; See A. Astraudo, *Saint-marin et l'Ordre de Malta*, LA REVUE DIPLOMATIQUE 7 (1935).

[453]Though the canon law of the Church accorded recognition to certain organisations.

[454]The best statement of this position – though dated – is that of J. HATSCHEK, AN OUTLINE OF INTERNATIONAL LAW trans C. Manning, 56 (1930), cited in D.P. O'CONNELL, INTERNATIONAL LAW, 85-86 (2d ed. 1970); Archbishop R. Martino, *A Short History of the Holy See's Diplomacy*, available at <http://www.holyseemission.org/short_history.html> (as at 1 December 2003).

The twentieth century, and particularly the second half of that century, saw the growth of international organisations and other bodies now accorded recognition as subjects in international law. With the growth in both the extent and the reach of international agreements, treaties, conventions and codes, the extent to which individual sovereign states retain the final control over their national policies may have diminished.[456] This tendency is becoming more noticeable in the modern commercial environment, and especially in respect of the Internet. The development of the Internet has presented new opportunities for those keen to escape the shackles of government. As yet, however, only states and international organisations that have been recognised as analogous are exempt from taxation by other states.[457]

The principal actor in international law is the state. If one cannot find a state whose fiscal and regulatory policies accord exactly with one's requirements, the option remains of creating one's own "ideal" state. Most of the attempts to create new states have been in oceanic or marine situations. The freedom and isolation of the open seas inhibit the control exercised by established powers, and encourage the formation of alternative political societies.[458] Menefee has identified four principal categories of territory that have been so used:

- the appropriation of apparently unclaimed islets (for example, Mead's state in the Spratly Islands);[459]

---

[455]Many countries (the U.S. and most Western European countries) did not recognise the incorporation of the Baltic States into the USS.R. in 1940, at least initially: U.S. Mission to the United Nations, *The United States reaffirms recognition of independence of Estonia, Latvia and Lithuania*, 29 July 1983, available at <http://web-static.vm.ee/static/failid/182/President_Reagan_statement.pdf> (as at 1 December 2003); cf G. Marston, *The British Acquisition of the Nicobar Islands, 1869: A Possible Example of Abandonment of Territorial Sovereignty*, 69 BRITISH YEARBOOK OF INTERN. LAW 245 (1998).

[456]Though even in the heyday of State sovereignty, the late 19th century, the extent to which any State was truly independent depended much on non-legal factors, such as relative economic strength.

[457]See Noel Cox, *Tax and regulatory avoidance through non-traditional alternatives to tax havens*, 9 NEW ZEALAND BUSINESS L. Q. 10-32 (2003).

[458]See S.P. Menefee, *Republics of the Reefs: Nation-Building on the Continental Shelf and in the World's Oceans*, 25 CALIFORNIA WESTERN INTERN. L. J. 81 (1994).

[459]See Noel Cox, *Tax and regulatory avoidance through non-traditional alternatives to tax havens*, 9 NEW ZEALAND BUSINESS L. Q. 10-32 (2003).

- the promulgation of sovereignty over reefs or low-tide elevations (for example, Grand and Triumph reefs);[460]
- the creation of states in shallow waters by dumping or other means (for example, Abalonia);[461] and
- the creation of states on totally artificial structures (for example, Sealand).[462]

Each of these categories presents particular difficulties for the would-be state-builder, whether that person be motivated by notions of unbridled free enterprise or libertarianism, or by pure eccentricity.[463]

But to be a state, a territory must have a permanent population,[464] it must have a defined territory,[465] it must have a government, and it must have the capacity to enter into diplomatic relations.[466] No other entity could

---

[460]See L. Horn, *To Be or Not to Be: The Republic of Minerva – Nation-founding by Individuals*, 12 COLUMBIA J. OF TRANSNATIONAL L. 520 (1973); S.P. Menefee, *Republics of the Reefs: Nation-Building on the Continental Shelf and in the World's Oceans*, 25 CALIFORNIA WESTERN INTERN. L. J. 81 (1994).

[461]See S.P. Menefee, *Republics of the Reefs: Nation-Building on the Continental Shelf and in the World's Oceans*, 25 CALIFORNIA WESTERN INTERN. L. J. 81 (1994).

[462]See N. PAPADAKIS, THE INTERNATIONAL LEGAL REGIME OF ARTIFICIAL ISLANDS (1977); S.P. Menefee, *Republics of the Reefs: Nation-Building on the Continental Shelf and in the World's Oceans*, 25 CALIFORNIA WESTERN INTERN. L. J. 81, 82 (1994).

[463]See Noel Cox, *Tax and regulatory avoidance through non-traditional alternatives to tax havens*, 9 NEW ZEALAND BUSINESS L. Q. 10-32 (2003).

[464]See the judgment of the International Court of Justice in the *Western Sahara*, Advisory Opinion, Intern. Court of Justice Reports 12, 63-65 (1975); 59 I.L.R. 30, 80-82.

[465]Which may however be very small, or even of varying extent: *United States v. Ray*, 281 F. Supp. 876 (S.D. Fla. 1965); *Atlantis Development Corporation v. United States*, 379 F. 2d 818 (5th Cir. 1967); *United States v. Ray*, 294 F. Supp. 532 (S.D. Fla. 1969); and *United States v. Ray*, 423 F. 2d 16 (5th Cir. 1970); *Chierici and Rosa v. Ministry of the Merchant Navy and Harbour Office of Rimini*, 71 I.L.R. 258 (14 November 1969) partial English translation and fact summary (citing (1975) 1 ITALIAN YEARBOOK OF INTERN. LAW 265 (Council of State); *In re Duchy of Sealand*, 80 I.L.R. 683 (1978) (Administrative Court of Cologne), cf <http://www.sealandgov.com> (as at 1 December 2003).

[466]This was expressly outlined in the Montevideo Convention on the Rights and Duties of States, 26 December 1933, 49 Stat. 3097; U.S.A. Treaty Series 881, entered into force on 26 December 1934, in 6 MANLEY OTTMER HUDSON (ed), INTERNATIONAL LEGISLATION, 620 (1931-50); available at

be regarded as a state, whatever its *de facto* power. This definition remains politically important, though additional factors have increased in relevance and importance.

Although the formal application of the Montevideo Convention is confined to Latin America, it is regarded as declaratory of customary international law.[467] The Arbitration Commission of the European Conference on Yugoslavia, in Opinion No 1, declared that:

> The state is commonly defined as a community which consists of a territory and a population subject to an organised political authority.[468]

No other entity could be regarded as a sovereign state, whatever its de facto power. But this does not mean that sovereign states alone enjoy a monopoly of power or authority.[469] As the concept of state sovereignty declined,[470] so notions of racial sovereignty have grown. The idea that a given population group is, or ought to be, sovereign within a larger country is not confined to any one country, such as New Zealand.[471] Yet, sovereign

---

<http://www.yale.edu/lawweb/avalon/intdip/interam/intam03.htm> (as at 1 December 2003). Although the formal application of the Convention is confined to Latin America, it is regarded as declaratory of customary international law. The Arbitration Commission of the European Conference on Yugoslavia, in Opinion No 1, declared that: "The state is commonly defined as a community which consists of a territory and a population subject to an organised political authority." (See 92 I.L.R. 162, 165). On the Arbitration Commission generally, see M. Craven, *The EC Arbitration Commission on Yugoslavia*, 66 BRITISH YEARBOOK OF INTERN. LAW 333 (1995).

[467]The Montevideo Convention on the Rights and Duties of States, signed 26 December 1933; 6 MANLEY OTTMER HUDSON (ed), INTERNATIONAL LEGISLATION, 620 (1931-50).

[468]92 Intern. Law Reports 162, 165. On the Arbitration Commission generally see M. Craven, *The EC Arbitration Commission on Yugoslavia*, 66 BRITISH YEARBOOK OF INTERN. LAW 333 (1995).

[469]See Noel Cox, *Tax and regulatory avoidance through non-traditional alternatives to tax havens*, 9 NEW ZEALAND BUSINESS L. Q. 10-32 (2003).

[470]In some countries it has also declined as a concept in domestic law, with an increased justiciability and limits upon sovereign immunity. See MAURICE SUNKIN AND SEBASTIAN PAYNE, THE NATURE OF THE CROWN: A LEGAL AND POLITICAL ANALYSIS (1999).

[471]For comparative purposes, see Richard Conley, SOVEREIGNTY OR THE STATUS QUO? THE 1998 PRE-REFERENDUM DEBATE IN QUEBEC, 35 J. OF COMMONWEALTH & COMP. POLITICS 67-92 (1997); Paul Howe, *Nationality*

states have clung tenaciously to their rights, rights which have become more precious as they become rarer.[472]

Even if a territory meets the Montevideo criteria, it will not necessarily be recognised by the international community. An old debate, between declaratory and constitutive theorists, centred on the role of recognition in transforming communities into states. Declaratory theorists asserted that recognition by existing states merely acknowledged that a community possessed the empirical attributes of a state – territory, population, a government, and the capacity to engage in international relations. Under this view, the function of recognition was merely to acknowledge that the state has come into existence and to signal a willingness to enter into diplomatic relations with the new state. Constitutive theorists, by contrast, considered recognition necessary to the creation of a new state. They further believed that recognition was a matter within the discretion of the recognising state to extend or withhold. The effect of the constitutive view is to hold a community's right to statehood hostage to the discretion of existing states.[473]

Grant considers the declaratory theory to be the better view, but he argues that neither view accurately describes the emergence of new states. Recent state practice renders the debate between declaratory and constitutive theory all the more inadequate. Some scholars have amended existing constitutive and declaratory theories by proposing additional requirements that communities must fulfil before becoming states, such as democratic governance or respect for minority rights. These additional rules, which have yet to gain widespread acceptance, pose additional difficulties in that they threaten to enlarge the scope of state discretion with respect to recognition. Grant contends that the alternative is to focus on the process that governs recognition rather than the substance of statehood.[474]

---

and Sovereignty Support in Quebec, 31 CANADIAN J. OF POLITICAL SCIENCE 31-60 (1998).

[472]For the impact of electronic commerce generally, see C.C. Nicoll, Electronic Commerce: a New Zealand perspective, 6 EDI L. REV.: LEGAL ASPECTS OF PAPERLESS COMMUNICATION 5-20 (1999).

[473]See C. Hillgruber, The Admission of New States to the International Community, 9 EUROPEAN J. OF INTERN. LAW 491 (1998), available at <http://www.ejil.org/J./Vol9/No3/ab3.html> (as at 1 December 2003).

[474]See T. GRANT, THE RECOGNITION OF STATES: LAW AND PRACTICE IN DEBATE AND EVOLUTION (1999). The European practice of recognising new States in Eastern Europe and in the former Soviet Union in 1991-1992 was based on the guidelines adopted by the European Commission Member States on 16 December 1991 (see 31 INTERN. LEGAL MATERIALS 1486 (1992)). The list of criteria lays down the conditions that had to be

A non-territorial state is perhaps possible.[475]

However far-fetched this possibility may be, we must reconsider the balance of international and domestic law. The jurisdiction of national courts is based upon the domestic laws of individual countries.[476] Similarly, the legislative jurisdiction of a state is limited to its territory.[477] The advent of cyberspace has not meant the decline of domestic law. But it has "pushed the boundaries."[478] Border controls on the Internet are not impossible to develop and implement.[479] Many governments already regulate cyberspace.[480] It may be that the most effective means to achieve

---

fulfilled before the Community was prepared to recognise the new States, and thus to agree to their admission to the community of States and to the international community. It has been claimed that the conditions listed in the guidelines are merely the criteria for the establishment of diplomatic relations – something which is in the political discretion of the States in any case – and not requirements for statehood in the sense of international law; M. Weller, *The International Response to the Dissolution of the Socialist Federal Republic of Yugoslavia*, 86 AM. J. OF INTERN. LAW 569, 588, 604 (1992). See also S. Talmon, *Recognition of Governments: An Analysis of the New British Policy and Practice*, 58 BRITISH YEARBOOK OF INTERN. LAW 231, 250-251 (1992).

[475]See Noel Cox, *Tax and regulatory avoidance through non-traditional alternatives to tax havens*, 9 NEW ZEALAND J. OF TAXATION L. & POLICY 305-327 (2003).

[476]See David R. Johnson & David G. Post, *Law and Borders: The Rise of Law in Cyberspace*, 48 STANFORD L. REV. 1367 (1996).

[477]See IAN BROWNLIE, PRINCIPLES OF PUBLIC INTERNATIONAL LAW, 301 (5th ed. 1998); 1 SIR ROBERT JENNINGS & SIR ARTHUR WATTS (eds), OPPENHEIM'S INTERNATIONAL LAW, 456 (9th ed. 1992); F.A. Mann, *The Doctrine of Jurisdiction in International Law*, 111 RECUEIL DES COURS 9, pp 10-13 (1964); F.A. Mann, *The Doctrine of Jurisdiction in International Law Revisited After Twenty Years*, 186(3) RECUEIL DES COURS 9, 20 (1984).

[478]See, for example, Tapio Puurunen, *The Legislative Jurisdiction of States over Transactions in International Electronic Commerce*, 18 JOHN MARSHALL J. OF COMPUTER & INFORM. L. 689 (2000).

[479]*United States v. Montoya de Hernandez*, 473 U.S. 531. See also Anne Wells Branscomb, *Jurisdictional Quandaries for Global Networks*, in LINDA M. HARASIM (ed), GLOBAL NETWORKS: COMPUTERS AND INFORMATIONAL COMMUNICATION, 83, 103 (1993).

[480]*Framework for Global Electronic Commerce*, available at <http://www.ecommerce.gov/> (as at 1 December 2003); *Management of Internet*, available at <http://www.ntia.doc.gov/> (as at 1 December 2003). Their legal right to do so is undoubted: *U.S. v. Smith*, 680 F. 2d 255 (1st Cir. Mass. 1982). See also President's Working Group on Unlawful Conduct on the Internet, *The Electronic Frontier: The Challenge of Unlawful Conduct Involving*

this is to regulate the architecture of cyberspace.[481] But for the most part the Internet is international; nor are its users adequately served by existing laws with respect to conflict of laws.[482] The efficacy of the private international law concept of the "closest and most real connection"[483] is also reduced, in that no part of the world is any more directly affected than any other by events on the web, as information is available simultaneously to anyone with a connection to the Internet.[484] Global computer-based communications cut across territorial borders,[485] creating a new realm of human activity and undermining the feasibility[486] – and legitimacy[487] – of

the Use of the Internet, March 2000, available at <http://www.usdoj.gov/criminal/cybercrime/unlawful.htm> (as at 1 December 2003).

[481]See Graham Greenleaf, *An Endnote on Regulating Cyberspace: Architecture vs Law?,* 21 U. NEW SOUTH WALES L. J. 593 (1998), available at <http://www.austlii.edu.au/au/other/unswlj.OLD/thematic/1998/vol21n o2/greenleaf.html> (as at 1 December 2003).

[482]The efficacy of the concept of "closest and most real connection" (*McConnell Dowell Constructors Ltd v. Lloyd's Syndicate 396,* 2 N.Z.L.R. 257 (1988) (CA)) is also reduced, in that no part of the world is any more directly affected than any other by events on the web, as information is available simultaneously to anyone with a connection to the Internet; David R. Johnson & David G. Post, *Law and Borders: The Rise of Law in Cyberspace,* 48 STANFORD L. REV. 1367 (1996). Nor, in terms of the protection of intellectual property rights: Dan L. Burk, *Muddy Rules for Cyberspace,* 21 CARDOZO L. REV. 121 (1998-99), available at <http://www.cardozo.yu.edu/cardlrev/v21n1/burk.pdf> (as at 1 December 2003).

[483]*McConnell Dowell Constructors Ltd v. Lloyd's Syndicate 396,* 2 N.Z.L.R. 257 (1988) (CA).

[484]See David R. Johnson & David G. Post, *Law and Borders: The Rise of Law in Cyberspace,* 48 STANFORD L. REV. 1367 (1996).

[485]Location remains important, but it is virtual location, rather than physical location. There is no necessary connection between an Internet address and a physical location. For a general description of the Domain Naming System, see D.L. Burk, *Trademarks Along the Infobahn: A First Look at the Emerging Law of Cybermarks,* 1 U. RICHMOND J. OF L. & TECHN. 1 (1995).

[486]Something which may be related to the relative length of the virtual border: see David R. Johnson & David G. Post, *Law and Borders: The Rise of Law in Cyberspace,* 48 STANFORD L. REV. 1367 (1996).

[487]With the dominance of democratic concepts of government, it might be thought that if the people believe that an institution is appropriate, then it is legitimate: Penelope Brook Cowen, *Neo Liberalism,* in RAYMOND MILLER

applying laws based on geographic boundaries.[488] Furthermore, the Internet threatens traditional political institutions and perhaps even the very concept of sovereignty itself.[489] As Zekos has written, the real jurisdictional novelty of cyberspace is that it will give rise to more frequent circumstances in which effects are felt in multiple territories at once.[490] Traditional international legal rules on jurisdiction do not fit the Internet context, nor do they facilitate cooperation on international regulation.

The legal right of countries to control the Internet is undoubted,[491] but the practical difficulties involved have been considerable. It may be that the most effective means to achieve this is to regulate the architecture of cyberspace[492] – but this is international. Perhaps more importantly, the

---

(ed), NEW ZEALAND POLITICS IN TRANSITION, 341 (1997). But this scheme leaves out of account substantive questions about the justice of the State and the protection it offers the individuals who belong to it. This point is illustrated by the study of the application of the model to Mummar Qadhafi's Libya: SALEH AL NAMLAH, POLITICAL LEGITIMACY IN LIBYA SINCE 1969, Syracuse Univ. PhD thesis (1992). It is generally more usual to maintain that a State's legitimacy depends upon its upholding certain human rights: JOHN RAWLS, POLITICAL LIBERALISM (1993); TED HONDERICH (ed), THE OXFORD COMPANION TO PHILOSOPHY, 477 "Legitimacy" (1995); M. SWANSON, THE SOCIAL EXTRACT TRADITION AND THE QUESTION OF POLITICAL LEGITIMACY, U. Missouri-Columbia PhD thesis 1995 (1995).

[488]See David R. Johnson & David G. Post, *Law and Borders: The Rise of Law in Cyberspace*, 48 STANFORD L. REV. 1361 (1996).

[489]See W. Lash, *The Decline of the Nation State in International Trade and Development*, CARDOZO L. REV. 1001 (1996-97); B. Sanford, *Teaching an Old Dog New Tricks*, 28 CONNECTICUT L. REV. 1137, 1170 (1995-96); D. Buck, *Patents in Cyberspace: Territoriality and Infringement on Global Computer Networks*, 68 TULANE L. REV. 1 (1993-94); W.B. WRISTON, THE TWILIGHT OF SOVEREIGNTY (1992) (examining the challenges to sovereignty posed by the information revolution).

[490]See Georgios Zekos, *Internet or Electronic Technology: A Threat to State Sovereignty*, 3 J. OF INFORM., L. & TECHN. (1999), available at <http://elj.warwick.ac.UK/jilt/99-3/zekos.html> (as at 28 November 2003).

[491]*U.S. v. Smith*, 680 F. 2d 255 (1st Cir. Mass. 1982). See also President's Working Group on Unlawful Conduct on the Internet, *The Electronic Frontier: The Challenge of Unlawful Conduct Involving the Use of the Internet*, March 2000, available at <http://www.usdoj.gov/criminal/cybercrime/unlawful.htm> (as at 1 December 2003).

advent of the Internet has encouraged debate as to the proper form of regulation of international trade. Should it be through separate legal systems generally conforming to certain norms, or should there be some form of international regulation? However, the speed of globalisation through the Internet means that the development of customary international law may not be sufficient to meet the needs of the new media – leaving international agreement or unilateral action as alternatives.

The notions of sovereignty and statehood are principally political concepts, rather than merely legal principles.[493] With the growth in both the (horizontal) extent and (vertical) reach of international agreements, treaties, conventions and codes, national independence is becoming less dominant. This tendency is becoming more noticeable in the modern commercial environment, and especially the Internet. For if electronic communication is (almost) instantaneous and global, who should regulate it and define its rules? Should it be subject to national regulation within some normative system – as the Law Merchant – or should it be recognised as a uniquely international system which requires international control?[494]

Further, the Internet itself threatens traditional political institutions and perhaps even the concept of sovereignty itself.[495] Traditional international legal rules on jurisdiction do not fit the Internet context, nor do they facilitate international co-operation on international regulation.

If sovereignty means the "final authority within a given territory",[496] then the contemporary growth of internationalisation, especially that brought about by the Internet, must have serious implications for state sovereignty.[497] Whilst the *lex mercatoria* impinged upon domestic sovereignty,

---

[492]See Graham Greenleaf, *An Endnote on Regulating Cyberspace: Architecture vs Law?*, 21 U. NEW SOUTH WALES L. J. 593 (1998), available at <http://www.austlii.edu.au/au/other/unswlj.OLD/thematic/1998/vol21n o2/greenleaf.html> (as at 1 December 2003).

[493]See S. Krasner, *Sovereignty: an institutional perspective*, 21 COMP. POLITICAL STUDIES 66-94 (1988).

[494]See Georgios Zekos, *Internet or Electronic Technology: A Threat to State Sovereignty*, 3 J. OF INFORM., L. & TECHN. (1999), available at <http://elj.warwick.ac.UK/jilt/99-3/zekos.html> (as at 28 November 2003).

[495]See W. Lash, *The Decline of the Nation State in International Trade and Development*, 18 CARDOZO L. REV. 1001 (1996-97); B. Sanford, *Teaching an Old Dog New Tricks*, 28 CONNECTICUT L. REV. 1137, 1170 (1995-96); D. Buck, *Patents in Cyberspace: Territoriality and Infringement on Global Computer Networks*, 68 TULANE L. REV. 1 (1993-94).

[496]See F. HINSLEY, SOVEREIGNTY (2d ed. 1996); S. Krasner, *Sovereignty: an institutional perspective*, 21 COMP. POLITICAL STUDIES 66-94 (1988).

in so far as this had developed in the early days of the law merchant, it did so to a limited extent. Perhaps more importantly, the law merchant evolved slowly, and did not impose an expectation of compliance upon any country.[498] It was, and is, a form of customary law. The existence of custom, unlike treaty-law, depends upon general agreement, not deliberate consent.[499] This requires time to develop, and is often uncertain. The Internet presents immediate problems, though not such as cannot be resolved through recourse to traditional legal principles and mechanisms. At present there is no reason to conclude that the Internet is in any sense a source of authority in its own right.[500] However, it has greatly accelerated the globalisation process, particularly with respect to trade, and as a consequence reduced the extent to which economic regulation remains in the hands of individual states. As a result of this the development of supra-states,[501] such as the European Union, is encouraged. This is a profoundly constitutional effect – and not one which relies on changes in society but is itself advancing ahead of social change – a case of capture by technology.

Lessons for the future – conceptualisation from previous examples of technological impact upon constitutions

What lessons may we take from these few examples of technological effects upon constitutions? Technology has influenced the state, and vice

---

[497]See Noel Cox, *The regulation of cyberspace and the loss of national sovereignty*, 11(3) INFORM. & COMMS. TECHN. L. 241-253 (2002).

[498]See LEON TRAKMAN, THE LAW MERCHANT – THE EVOLUTION OF COMMERCIAL LAW (1983).

[499]See GERHARD VON GLAHN, LAW AMONG NATIONS: AN INTRODUCTION TO PUBLIC INTERNATIONAL LAW (7th ed. 1996).

[500]Though it has been argued that it should be; See David R. Johnson & David G. Post, *Law and Borders: The Rise of Law in Cyberspace*, 48 STANFORD L. REV. 1367 (1996); David R. Johnson & David G. Post, *And How Shall the Net be Governed? A Meditation on the Relative Virtues of Decentralised, Emergent Law*, draft paper at Cyberspace Law Institute Papers on Cyberspace Law, 1996, available at <http://www.cli.org/emdraft.html> (as at 28 November 2003). Geist, Reidenberg, and others have rejected this notion; See, for example, Joel R. Reidenberg, *Governing Networks and Rule-making in Cyberspace*, 45 EMORY L. J. 922 (1996); Joel R. Reidenberg, *Lex Informatica: The Formulation of Information Policy Rules Through Technology*, 76 TEXAS L. REV. 553 (1998).

[501]A supra-state, not a super-state, because it is not a state but rather a political entity linking existing states.

versa. Every few centuries, there has been a seminal shift in the balance of society, technology, and constitution. Those counties which were unable to adjust declined,[502] those that made the adjustment prospered.[503] These could perhaps indicate that a state must harness technology, not be harnessed by it, in order to succeed – which raises questions about the interrelationship of private enterprise and capital, and the state.

Each of the these technological and historical periods was marked by quite different technological, economic, social, political and constitutional features. In some cases, such as Egypt, the Reformation, and during the Industrial Revolution, it is comparatively easy to see how technological change effected society, and therefore the constitution. Even in the Roman empire, and during the Middle Ages, there were signs that this was also occurring. That technology changes society, society changes the constitution, may be a commonplace. But we can see signs that technology has directly affected the constitution, while also having social or economic effects.

Some technological changes have directed effected the constitution, others have not. Seminal changes which have a direct impact of the structure of the constitution may be rare, but it may be that we are facing one now. The difference between technological changes in the past and those now is a matter of pace rather than essential nature. The changes are so rapid – particularly the Internet and the move to globalisation – that it is scarcely possible for a state to resist it. This has an effect upon the relationship of states, and the ways in which domestic laws are made.

Not only has, to use the U.S. example, the balance between federal and state powers changed – in McGinnis' view because of the advent of telecommunications[504] – but the Internet is potentially capable of undermining state identity and cohesion.[505] This is due to the availability of the Internet to millions of relatively ordinary citizens.

But at a different level, that of international trade, the division between states has also been weakened. Traditionally, the formation of legal norms for conducting trade was by states, subject to certain customary principles accepted by the international community. But this has proven inadequate for the control of electronic commerce, because this can be said to be truly international, having no physical presence, and the development has been too swift to allow for the evaluation of customary norms.

The new environment has necessitated an increased degree of

---

[502]For example, Egypt during the Second Intermediate Period.
[503]Ad did the U.K. during the Industrial Revolution.
[504]See John O. McGinnis, *The Symbiosis of Constitutionalism and Technology*, 25 HARV. J. OF L. & PUBL. POLICY 3, 6 (2001).
[505]See CASS R. SUNSTEIN, REPUBLIC.COM (2001).

international co-ordination, if not co-operation. Unlike the evolutionary development of the *lex mercatoria*, the advent of electronic communications has resulted in the adoption of international norms, such as the UNCITRAL Model Law on Electronic Commerce.

This does pose a threat to state sovereignty. It is no longer possible for the nation-state to be the sole, or even prime, regulator of economic norms. Decisions respecting the forms of law will be made not at the national level, but internationally. These will be made by political blocks, and, in some instances, by non-governmental organisations. There are wider implications for national legal systems which cannot be ignored.

A prediction made some years ago that the Internet would change international law because it would erode the dominance of the traditional sovereign state[506] has not become reality yet. But it is potentially a threat to state sovereignty,[507] and therefore of profound constitutional implications. The knowledge revolution is likely to be as revolutionary in effect as was the Reformation. But this may well be over a much longer period of time than some might have expected, and it is likely to be in the international field rather than the domestic. For the prime determinant of statehood is war – the laws of war (now called those of armed conflict) are still important, and they have not been subjected to the same degree of globalisation.[508] The security of the state – as perceived by state authorities – will continue to determine policy.[509]

---

[506]See Henry H. Perritt, *The Internet is Changing International Law*, 73 CHICAGO-KENT L. REV. 997 (1998).

[507]See Georgios Zekos, *Internet or Electronic Technology: A Threat to State Sovereignty*, 3 J. OF INFORM., L. & TECHN. (1999), available at <http://elj.warwick.ac.UK/jilt/99-3/zekos.html> (as at 28 November 2003); David G. Post & David R. Johnson, *'Chaos Prevailing on Every Continent': Towards a New Theory of Decentralised Decision-Making in Complex Systems*, 14 June 1999, Social Science Research Network Electronic Library, available   at <http://papers.ssrn.com/sol3/delivery.cfm/99032613.pdf?abstractid=157 692> (as at 1 December 2003). See also Dan L. Burk, *Federalism in Cyberspace*, 28 CONNECTICUT L. REV. 1095 (1996); Joel R. Reidenberg, *Governing Networks and Rule-Making in Cyberspace*, in BRIAN KAHIN & CHARLES NESSON (eds), BORDERS IN CYBERSPACE, 84, 85-87 (1997).

[508]Though there have been major advances in the course of the latter part of the nineteenth century and the twentieth century – influenced not a little by technology (the threat of chemical, biological, and nuclear weapons, for example); See ADAM ROBERTS & RICHARD GUELFF (eds), LAWS OF WAR (2000); GEOFFREY BEST, HUMANITY IN WARFARE: THE MODERN HISTORY OF THE INTERNATIONAL LAW OF ARMED CONFLICT (1980).

It would appear that modern high technology does affect the constitution, but mostly indirectly. Its most significant effect is in the international sphere, and this particularly important given the globalising effect of current technological developments.

---

[509]See, for instance, the USA Patriot Act of 2001, Public Law 107-56.

CONCLUSIONS

It has been suggested by Scheuerman that we should see constitutions as expressive of a broadly-defined set of abstract moral principles, along the lines proposed by Dworkin.[510] These may be challenged by changing social norms, brought about by the Internet and by globalisation in general, or by other technological changes. The case of the US Constitution suggests that rigidity in formal amendment procedures[511] might be compensated for by flexibility within constitutional exegesis.[512] For Justice Cardozo observed that "nothing is stable. Nothing absolute. All is fluid and changeable. We are back with Heraclitus."[513] This situation, for him, defied formalistic modes of constitutional exegesis. He believed that judges therefore should adopt a "more plastic, more malleable" reading of the U.S. Constitution in order to guarantee its relevance to the changing exigencies of the times.[514]

---

[510]William E. Scheuerman, *Constitutionalism in an age of speed*, 19 CONSTITUTIONAL COMMENTARY 353, 366 (2002).

[511]The U.S. Constitution contains a system of amendment now widely seen as one of the most slow-going in the world; See JAMES L. SUNDQUIST, CONSTITUTIONAL REFORM AND EFFECTIVE GOVERNMENT, 17 (1992); Donald S. Lutz, *Toward a Theory of Constitutional Amendment*, in SANFORD LEVINSON (ed), RESPONDING TO IMPERFECTION, 237 (1995). For amendment processes generally, see KEITH G. BANTING & RICHARD SIMEON (eds), REDESIGNING THE STATE: THE POLITICS OF CONSTITUTIONAL CHANGE (1985).

[512]See JAMES BRYCE, CONSTITUTIONS, 72-73 (1901).

[513]BENJAMIN N. CARDOZO, THE NATURE OF THE JUDICIAL PROCESS, 28 (1921). Heraclitus said that nothing is stable, that permanence is an illusion conceived by man, and that strife "is the justice of the world ... "; EDUARD ZELLER, OUTLINES OF THE HISTORY OF GREEK PHILOSOPHY trans L.R. Palmer, 46 (13th ed. 1948).

[514]BENJAMIN N. CARDOZO, THE NATURE OF THE JUDICIAL PROCESS, 161

This approach is likely to be satisfactory to respond to the domestic influences of technological change. But in the international – or transnational effects of technological change that approach may not be sufficient.

One alternative is the parliamentary constitution, on the U.K. or New Zealand model, in which constitutional changes may be made by ordinary legislation.[515] This allows, for example, the U.K. to steadily increase its constitutional relationship with the European Union, without the necessity for a referendum.[516] Whichever model is preferred, we can see that the measure of success is that the disparity between constitutional forms and social, economic and political realities do not become so great that the viability of the state is imperilled.

From the earliest times, through the Middle Ages, the Reformation, and to the present, technology has affected the constitution indirectly, through its effects upon society and economy. Yet, there have been significant technologies which have proven to be of great importance in shaping the nature of the constitution. Whether this was by fostering a centralised system of government, or the opposite, the effect must be seen as more than merely indirect. Success came to those states which were able to respond most quickly to the changing environment in which it found itself. Sometimes – as in the Industrial Revolution – this meant taking a more active role than hitherto. Failure to act resulted in economic stagnation.[517]

With the present technological revolution bringing about globalisation at an unparalleled rate it would appear to be essential for states to take the

---

(1921).

[515]In Ackerman's terminology, the model of constitutional change represents the paradigmatic case of "constitutional monism" for which "the British design captures the essence of democracy"; 1 BRUCE ACKERMAN, WE THE PEOPLE, 8 (1991).

[516]See KENNETH DYSON & KEVIN FEATHERSTONE, THE ROAD TO MAASTRICHT: NEGOTIATING ECONOMIC AND MONETARY UNION (1999). There was, however, a referendum on whether the U.K. should remain a member, shortly after joining the then European Community, in 1975; STANLEY ALDERSON, YEA OR NAY?: REFERENDA IN THE UNITED KINGDOM (1975).

[517]For instance, in the Iberian countries, in which the Reformation was less profound then elewhere, partly because constitutional rigidity led to restrictions in the development and adoption of technology – and a general ediucational backwardness – for many years; See Richard L. Kagan, *Students and society in early modern Spain* (Johns Hopkins University Press, Baltimore, 1974).

initiative, rather than merely respond to what others have done. The potential changes are such that the revolution may be seen as paradigmatic. Failure to act will render states subservient to changes beyond their control. The difficulty is in determining what changes are needed. Constitutional reforms which accellerate the process for the enactment of international agreements, and the removal of any which inhibit the extraterritorial jurisdiction of national courts, might be worthwhile.

ABOUT THE AUTHOR

Noel Cox was born in Auckland, New Zealand. After attending grammar school in Takapuna, he took up the study of law at the University of Auckland (where he obtained an LL.B.). After graduation he was admitted as a Barrister and Solicitor of the High Court of New Zealand, and later practised as a Barrister. He undertook an LL.M. at the same university, and received the Fowlds Memorial Prize as most distinguished student in the Faculty of Law. He subsequently undertook a Ph.D. His doctoral research was in the fields of law and political studies, and was on the topic of the "The Evolution of the New Zealand Monarchy: The Recognition of an Autochthonous Polity". This was extensively revised and expanded and published as *A Constitutional History of the New Zealand Monarchy: The evolution of the New Zealand monarchy and the recognition of an autochthonous polity* (Verlag Dr. Müller Aktiengesellschaft & Co. K.G., Saarbrücken, 2008).

He also holds an M.A. of the Archbishop of Canterbury's Examination in Theology, for a canon law thesis – supervised by Professor Norman Doe, of Cardiff Law School's Centre of Law and Religion – entitled "An exploration of the basis of legal authority of the Anglican Church in New Zealand". This was later fully revised and expanded and was published as *Church and State in the Post-Colonial Era: The Anglican Church and the Constitution in New Zealand* (Polygraphia (NZ) Ltd, Auckland, 2008). He also completed a Licence in Theology (L.Th.) from the University of Wales Lampeter (the former St David's College, now the University of Wales Trinity Saint David). He subsequently completed an M.Theol. at the University of Auckland, in the field of systematic theology, with a thesis on the topic of "The meaning of catholicity with respect to ordained ministry in the Anglican Communion: An examination of the ecclesiology implicit in the validity of orders debate". He obtained a Certificate in Tertiary Teaching (Cert.Tert.Tchg.), and a Graduate Diploma in Tertiary Teaching

(Grad.Dip.Tert.Tchg.), from the Auckland University of Technology, where he commenced his career as an academic lawyer.

Noel Cox holds the position of Professor of Law at Aberystwyth University. He was Head of the Department of Law and Criminology 2010-2013. He was Professor of Constitutional Law (and inaugural professor of law) at the Auckland University of Technology to 2010, where he was formerly the Head of the Department of Law. He received the Vice-Chancellor's Excellence Award for Research, of the Auckland University of Technology, in 2002. Professor Cox spent the summer of 2003-2004 as a Visiting Fellow in the Faculty of Law of The Australian National University, Canberra (later leading to the publication of *Technology and Legal Systems* (Ashgate Publishing Ltd, Aldershot, 2006)), and the latter part of 2006 at Wolfson College, the University of Cambridge (leading to *Constitutional paradigms and the stability of states* (Ashgate Publishing Ltd, Aldershot, 2012)). In 2009 he was elected Visiting Fellow at St Edmund's College, University of Cambridge, though he was not able to take this up as he then accepted appointment to Aberystwyth University.

Apart from New Zealand, he is also admitted to practice law in almost all the Australian jurisdictions (the Australian Capital Territory, New South Wales, the Northern Territory, Queensland, South Australia, Tasmania and Victoria). He was called to the bar of England and Wales, by the Honourable Society of the Inner Temple.

He was previously Chairman of Monarchy New Zealand (formerly The Monarchist League of New Zealand), and also a member of the Council of the Auckland District Law Society. He is a Fellow of the Royal Historical Society, as well as of the Burgon Society (for the study of academic dress). As part of his interest in academic dress he wrote *Academical Dress in New Zealand* (Verlag Dr. Müller Aktiengesellschaft & Co. K.G., Saarbrücken, 2010).

He was an ordinand in the Diocese of Auckland, New Zealand, and was ordained a deacon and then a priest in the Diocese of St Davids of the Church in Wales, after undertaking training at St Michael and All Angels Theological College, Llandaff, whilst serving a placement in the parish of Llanbadarn Fawr, Aberystwyth, where he is now serving his title as Assistant Curate, now in the Group Benefice of Llanbadarn Fawr, Elerch with Penrhyn-coch with Capel Bangor.

He is married.

Previous books, including those mentioned above, include *Selected Sermons, 2009-2013* (Ardwyn House Publishing, Aberystwyth, 2014), *Four months in Europe: A New Zealand academic at large* (Ardwyn House Publishing, Aberystwyth, 2014), *Theological Reflections: Some thoughts on the road to ordination* (Ardwyn House Publishing, Aberystwyth, 2014), *Collected Essays: Part 1* (Ardwyn House Publishing, Aberystwyth, 2014), *Collected Essays: Part 2*

(Ardwyn House Publishing, Aberystwyth, 2014), *Sir Henry Rider Haggard: A collection of commentaries on his novels* (CreateSpace Independent Publishing Platform, 2013), *The Enforcement of Professional Ethics and Standards in the Kenyan Legal Profession* (The World Bank/The Law Society of Kenya, Nairobi, 2007, revised 2013 CreateSpace Independent Publishing Platform, 2013), *Essays on Constitutional Law: with particular emphasis on the Crown* (CreateSpace Independent Publishing Platform, 2013*)*, *The law of the church in the twenty-first century: Essays on law and religion* (CreateSpace Independent Publishing Platform, 2013), *Constitutional paradigms and the stability of states* (Ashgate Publishing Ltd, Aldershot, 2012), *Academical Dress in New Zealand* (Verlag Dr. Müller Aktiengesellschaft & Co. K.G., Saarbrücken, 2010), *The catholicity of ordained ministry in the Anglican Communion: An examination of the ecclesiology implicit in the validity of orders debate* (V.D.M. Verlag Dr. Müller Aktiengesellschaft & Co. K.G., Saarbrücken, 2009), *Church and State in the Post-Colonial Era: The Anglican Church and the Constitution in New Zealand* (Polygraphia (NZ) Ltd, Auckland, 2008), *A Constitutional History of the New Zealand Monarchy: The evolution of the New Zealand monarchy and the recognition of an autochthonous polity* (Verlag Dr. Müller Aktiengesellschaft & Co. K.G., Saarbrücken, 2008) and *Technology and Legal Systems* (Ashgate Publishing Ltd, Aldershot, 2006).

He is the author of more than 200 academic papers, primarily in the fields of constitutional law, legal history, and ecclesiastical law.

www.ingramcontent.com/pod-product-compliance
Lightning Source LLC
Chambersburg PA
CBHW051734170526
45167CB00002B/931